Collins

Successful Networking

IN

7

SIMPLE STEPS

Collins

HarperCollins Publishers
77-85 Fulham Palace Road
Hammersmith
London W6 8JB

First edition 2014
Reprint 10 9 8 7 6 5 4 3 2 1 0
© HarperCollins Publishers 2014
ISBN 978-0-00-750717-7
Collins ® is a registered trademark of HarperCollins Publishers Limited.
www.collinselt.com
A catalogue record for this book is available from the British Library.
Typeset in India by Aptara
Printed and bound in Great Britain by Clays Ltd, St Ives plc

The Publisher and author wish to thank the following rights holders for the use of copyright material. With thanks to Twitter for the use of Twitter and Tweet.
Every effort has been made to contact the holders of copyright material, but if any have been inadvertently overlooked, the Publisher will be pleased to make the necessary arrangements at the first opportunity.
Illustrations by Scott Garrett

MIX
Paper from
responsible sources
FSC™ C007454
FSC
www.fsc.org

FSC™ is a non-profit international organisation established to promote the responsible management of the world's forests. Products carrying the FSC label are independently certified to assure consumers that they come from forests that are managed to meet the social, economic and ecological needs of present and future generations, and other controlled sources.

Find out more about HarperCollins and the environment at
www.harpercollins.co.uk/green

Contents

About the author

Clare Dignall has worked in both the public and private sectors, in established organizations and challenging start-ups. Since working for herself, she has realized – more so than ever – the importance of forming close business relationships and extending her network. When authoring this book, Clare used material from Barry Tomalin's *Key Business Skills* (HarperCollins 2012) in addition to bouncing ideas off Joe Cairney of *Projects on Track*, who Clare would like to thank for his insights and enthusiasm. Clare is also the author of Collins' *Can You Eat, Shoot & Leave?*, the official companion to Lynne Truss's bestseller *Eats, Shoots & Leaves*, as well as Collins' *Negotiation Skills in 7 Simple Steps*.

CREATING NETWORKING OPPORTUNITIES

'The richest people in the world look for and build networks, everyone else looks for work.'
— Robert T. Kiyosaki, Author

Five ways to succeed

- Know your reasons for networking.

- Re-acquaint yourself with people you already know.

- Value both close friends and acquaintances.

- Give, without expecting anything in return.

- Learn how to measure your networking results.

Five ways to fail

- Don't waste time networking with family.

- Try to make as many new contacts as you possibly can.

- Get what you want out of every meeting.

- Let your networking take its own natural course.

- Network as soon as you can: sort out business detail later.

Where do I start?

Networking. Everyone talks about it. But what on earth is networking anyway? Simply put, networking is the process of meeting new people, and maintaining valuable contact with these people, to the benefit of both you and them. It's not a special business skill, it's a human and social aptitude that we all have. But one of the most important things that can shape your networking, is knowing what you want out of it. Take a minute to consider the following:

- Am I networking in order to change career?

- Do I want to start networking after a career break?

- Am I networking in order to grow my own business?

- Am I networking to grow the client base of the company I work for?

If you want to change career, for example, you should be attempting to 'break out' of your existing network to source new contacts. Conversely, if you're growing your own business, you may want to network in a focused way within one specific target market. Whatever your approach, remember this – networking presents opportunities in unexpected places, so never be closed to a serendipitous meeting, even if it is not in your 'game plan'.

Identifying your existing network

You may be thinking 'How can I network if I don't even *have* a network?' Well the good news is, you do, and it probably looks something like this:

- **Your family:** a reliable source of support, information and local knowledge.

- **Your friends:** people you rely on for support and ideas.

- **Your work or study colleagues, past or present:** people who know your work skills can give insights into other roles that might suit you, and possibly new vacancies.

- **Your acquaintances:** people you meet day-to-day – your barber, mechanic, neighbour etc.

Surprisingly, it's the people you know least that could be most useful to you. Known as 'weak ties', these people are at the edges of your social network, so know a different set of people who may present fresh opportunities. The trick in successful networking is to invest time in these weak ties to ensure that, should an opportunity arise, it is your name that they think of first.

Rediscovering your existing network

So, you already have a personal network in place. As yet, it may be untapped. To breathe new life into this existing network, you need do little more than set aside some time and adopt a new way of thinking. All of us are guilty to some extent of dismissing the people we know 'Oh that's Mike, I worked with him in IT, bit of a web geek' and leaving them languishing in the little stereotypes we've dumped them in. If you're serious about networking it's time to look at everyone you know with fresh eyes. What are their skills you don't you know about? What are their hobbies? What are their aspirations? Who do they work with? What do they believe are your best talents? Spend time with friends, family and colleagues you've not seen lately. Make an effort not to hog conversation or go over old topics. Treat them as if you've just met. Listen (you'll find insights into how to do this in Step 4). You'll be amazed at what you will unearth.

Similarly, when you're getting a haircut or doing the school run, don't ignore everyone because you think the people you meet at these times are not 'important'. Engage them in conversation, allow them to talk. Listen. Hey presto – you're networking. Networking is a way of life; it affects and underlines the value of our interactions with all human beings – you can't just save it for the moments labelled 'Networking Event'.

Blood may not be thicker than water

When you are building an effective and supportive network it is important to know exactly who you can rely on in a tight spot. We have all heard the old saying 'blood is thicker than water' and many of us assume that our strongest ties are those that are related to us through blood or marriage. But in the world of business, it is often safest to assume nothing. It can be enlightening, at regular periods, to ask yourself the following questions:

■ Am I happy with who is closest to me?

When we talk about the people that are 'closest' to us, we usually include family and long-standing friends in that list. They are the people who have known us the longest, we spend most time with, and in most instances, have partially 'created' the person that we are now through long years of parenting, peer interaction, schooling and socializing. We unquestioningly assume they are on our side. But are they? Time to ask yourself a tough question: 'Am I still happy with how much my family and friends influence me?' Perhaps you seek the approval of parents or friends a little too much? Are your peers suspicious of success? Are you staying in a job you don't want because you feel that's what's expected of you? If your aim to is to change the way your life looks, you may have to work out whether there are any people, very close to you, that are limiting you.

■ **Who would I turn to in a crisis?**

It's likely that asking yourself the first question will have revealed some unsettling home truths. By asking just one more tough question, you *will* find out who your real friends are. Imagine yourself in an awful situation. You've lost your job, your business is failing, or you're going through a gruelling period of stress at work. Who, in reality, would you turn to? Without analysing too much, quickly write down a list of the people you would turn to first for advice and help. You may be surprised by what you see. If some of the entries on that list are people that you would never have counted as strong ties – are not family, and whom you see rarely, it may be time to sort that out. These people are clearly important to you on many levels: make it a priority to invest some time in them now. If you ever are to be faced with that worst-case scenario, you want them wholly on your side.

By asking two simple questions, you are likely to have a much clearer idea about who you want 'on your team'. Some people are just plain good for us – they are supportive, trustworthy, positive and inspiring – in their company we aspire to greater things. Some people are not so good for us and can seriously limit what we can achieve. The trick is identifying who is who, and we'll find out more later.

Using your existing network

A big reason for many people beginning to network seriously is that they want 'change'. Well, you can start the process of change, and build your confidence too, just from the people you already know.

Build bridges to other networks

One very simple way to give your network's breadth an immediate boost is to hold your own event. Make it an 'open house' and ask your friends to bring a few of their friends. This is a simple way to stretch the edges of your network and open pathways to new ones. Be attentive to the new faces amongst your guests – they will remember a good listener and may end up being valuable contacts or friends.

Surround yourself with those that bring out your best

Ever noticed that you always look better in photos taken with your best friends? It doesn't apply to just our looks; people that are 'good' for us bring out the best in us – our best work, ideas and attitude. If you want positive change, start spending most time with the people in your network that make you feel good. This simple tactic can have a positive effect on your outlook and self-confidence.

Creating brand-new networks

So, you are mining all the value of your existing network by rediscovering the people in it and making new mutual acquaintances. Now add some new faces by breaking out of your existing network entirely. But how?

- **Visit your library:** Your local library holds information on business and social events in your area, and many of these will be free.

- **Business support organizations:** Organizations like Business Link in England and Business Gateway in Scotland offer free and impartial advice to people in business or starting their own. Many run free workshops so you can learn new skills and meet like-minded people at the same time.

- **Research online:** Type in the keywords of your field of interest or business and search for upcoming events. You'll soon find something within feasible travelling distance that suits your budget.

- **Night classes and courses:** If you are planning to change careers or are coming back to work you may need to acquire a new set of skills. Short courses refresh your CV and your network too.

- **Volunteering:** Want to learn new skills, meet new people and on a tight budget? Find your nearest volunteering centre and ask them about opportunities.

Quality as well as quantity

It's generally believed that a person can only sustain around 150 meaningful social relationships; all those people you see on Facebook with 350+ friends don't really have 350 lifelong buddies; they'll have a few, the rest are acquaintances.

Ensure that your growing network has 'balance' too. Is it made up of both strong ties (people you can rely on) and weak ties (acquaintances who may present an opportunity in the future)? If one group dominates, then it may be time to redress the balance. Reid Hoffman, Co-Founder and Chairman of LinkedIn®, makes a helpful analogy to explain this process of finding 'balance': you have one memory card for your digital camera on a six-month trip. Because the capacity is finite, you must choose whether you want to store a few great photos at hi-res, store hundreds at lo-res, or a mixture of both. So it is with your network – you cannot maintain all your relationships at 'hi-res', but a huge, 'lo-res' network will not provide you with the support you need when times are hard. You need a mixture of both: strong ties to help and guide you on your career journey, and weak ties to refresh your network, provide new information and offer opportunities.

Examine your attitude

You may not yet be convinced by the idea of networking. Many people still have a suspicion of networking, associating it with dishonesty and aggressive deal-making. For some misguided souls, that's what networking is: only coming out of the office when you need something, working the event to get the introduction you want, or squeezing your new contact till you get the deal you want. Effective in the short term, but you'll make no lasting relationships.

Contemporary approaches to networking turn this short-sighted tactic on its head. It's all about building lasting relationships first, and, crucially, offering upfront value to your new contact in the hope that someday you may reap reward in return. This kind of networker ('go-givers' in networking terminology) will meet new people and attempt to see the world from their eyes, listening to their needs and aspirations. He or she will then consider whether they might be of help to the other person to fulfil those needs. Could they introduce someone useful? Do they have some information they could share? This 'help' just has to be timely, appropriate, and of value to the other. Establishing relationships on these grounds will gain you lifelong allies.

Becoming event-ready

Now let's check that we are 'event-ready' from an entirely practical perspective. You may have the best attitude in the world but to be a successful networker you will also have to prepare in other ways: what do you need to take with you? Do you need a business card? Do you really need to finish your website before you tell people about it? What practical preparations do we need to make to network at events effectively? In the coming pages we consider some useful practical preparations.

Get business cards printed

Although we live in a hi-tech, increasingly paperless age, it's a surprising fact that the business card is still a must-have item in the world of networking. The act of exchanging them is a rite of passage in itself, a sort of low-level 'trade and contract' between you and the person you've just met. The reciprocal movement of exchange also provides a physical ice-breaker and puts the two of you on a level playing field.

If you are networking on behalf of your employer, it's likely you already have a business card. If you don't, you need to get some, for without business cards, all your networking efforts will be for naught. If you are starting your own business then ensure you have business cards printed before you start networking. You may think that's a start-up expense you could do without, but it's imperative to have some and they needn't cost much – the web is full of sites printing business cards at very little cost. If you are hoping to switch careers, you may want to consider printing a personal business card, so that you can prevent a job offer being sent to a work email. What's on your business card? Remember, you may need more information for use internationally than you need in your own country. And you may need information in the language of the country in which you plan to network.

Petersfield Projects

pp

Tony Fawkes M.A.
Managing Director

Petersfield Projects
6 Manor Drive, Petersfield, Sussex PO3 2PZ

T   01377 201564
M 097015 400400
E   tony.fawkes@petersfieldprojects.co.uk
W www.petersfieldprojects.co.uk

Check your 'back office'

Before you finalize your business cards, ensure that everything you say on the card holds true. There is nothing more infuriating than typing in a web address from a business card and finding that the website is a work in progress, or (much worse) cannot be found. Such a faux pas will speak undesirable volumes about your organizational skills, so before you give out business cards, literally do what a new contact would do. Get someone to ring your phone number and ensure that it comes directly to you, send a test email to the address printed (especially if it's new), and double-check that the web address printed is operational. It's amazing how many people get this terribly wrong – with permanent and disastrous results.

Do you have the appropriate kit?

Networking relies mostly on your ability to listen and converse. However, if you are in a particularly visual field of business, you may want to use equipment to help illustrate what you do. The key here is making the technology work for you, not against you. It's going to be easier to talk over a tablet than waiting for a laptop to boot up (and necessitate sitting). Do you have comfortable and professional-looking means of carrying whatever equipment you need? Can you get it in and out of its bag easily without interrupting conversation? Think about the reality of bringing hardware into a networking situation with you. It has to look good, look easy and appropriate.

What should be on your business card?

If you have a choice about what goes on your business card, you can make it say a lot about you, or the nature of your business. Be creative, but remember that the business card is an important document:

- **Provide your contact details:** Provide your name and your job title. Then provide your (or your company's) address, telephone number, email address and web address.

- **Use a horizontal orientation:** Using a landscape rather than a portrait orientation will ensure you will have space to enter your full contact details.

- **Use a standard size:** The standard A8 or 74 x 52 mm is the desired size. Annoying business cards that won't fit neatly in a standard wallet or card holder will not be filed properly by recipients and could get lost.

- **Left align all text for maximum readability:** Centred text can look naïve and unprofessional, and it obstructs readability.

- **Use one font:** Stick to one font (and its related italic/bold if necessary) to prevent your business card from looking disorganized.

- **Check and double-check:** Proofread your business card thoroughly, and ask a friend to do the same, before you send it to print. One typo in your phone number can result in a very quiet business year if you don't notice it.

- **Less is more:** Don't aim to provide any in-depth company or personal information. At the very most, you could include a strapline. You will be doing the talking, not the business card. Look again at the business card on page 16 as an example.

Planning your networking

You must put effort into planning your networking. Like any other project, you need to plan it, schedule it and monitor success. That way, you'll spot blind alleys before time and effort is wasted, freeing you up to follow more promising leads. How you plan such a personal thing as networking is up to you. You might create a spreadsheet and enter in your goals, activities, and resulting business in it, with scheduled alerts to meet new contacts regularly. You might create a mind map connecting people and ideas in a more organic way. The choice is yours, but a few key questions will shape that plan:

- What do I want to achieve for myself and my business in the long term?

- Who do I want to meet to help me achieve that?

- How much time/money can I spend per month?

- What are my immediate networking goals at each event?

- How do I measure my networking success?

- Do I need different tactics for different groups?

You will have many of your own questions to add to the above, but this list may give you ideas as to how you might plan your own networking successfully.

Three tools for network planning

If you are under pressure with work or the launch of your own business, you may feel that networking doesn't feel 'mission-critical' enough to waste time in its planning. If that sounds like you, then three simple tools could help you manage your networking effectively:

- **Scheduling:** Set aside a time each week or month to plan and review your networking and block this time off in your diary. That way, you won't feel that you must 'find' time amongst your other commitments – you already have it set aside. Schedule these sessions for days when you know you'll need a break from other projects; thinking about networking and the opportunities it can bring can be a good motivator if other things aren't going your way. If it's in your diary, you won't be tempted to skip planning either – networking without clear goals can be haphazard and costly.

- **Funding:** If you are starting your own business, or are networking for personal development, it's a good idea to factor in a monthly allowance for networking. It's positive to think of this as a necessary start-up cost, rather than an expense you can ill afford – you want to be able to catch up with contacts for coffees and lunches without feeling that you are dipping into earnings. If a once in a lifetime opportunity comes up, having some travel funds in place means you can enjoy the experience, rather than arrive stressed-out about your bank balance and resentful of the whole affair.

■ **Measuring:** Critical to your networking planning is finding a way to measure how you're doing. Which network events result in the greatest number of active contacts? What are my monthly networking expenses against new business generated directly from it? Which contacts do I spend most time with and are we deriving mutual benefit? Does local networking yield more useful contacts than travelling to events further afield? You may ask any number of questions like this to identify how your networking is 'delivering', or combine them to interrogate your results effectively. Over time, you will build up a picture of the events, places and people that are most useful to you now, and others that may become more useful later. Asking questions helps you get the 'big picture' of the path you are taking through your networking career, and crucially, how to take charge of planning it.

Avoiding hiccups on the day

There's nothing quite like preparation to smooth your way into an event. Many of the following pointers apply to travel anywhere, but never more so than to a network event where it's imperative you arrive looking cool, calm and collected.

Do you really know where you're going?

It's likely that you will attend network events in places you don't know, and saying 'I'm sure I will find it okay' won't do if you are going to avoid getting lost. On the night before, identify your route on a paper or online map and locate the nearest bus stops, stations or car parks.

Time your travel to the minute

If you want to ensure that you arrive promptly before cliques start to form you must research how long it's going to take you to get there. Does the event start during the morning or evening rush hour? You'll need to factor in extra time for travel. Is there public transport or parking nearby? Some posh events may be held in places that are 'traffic-free'. In such cases you may have to allow time for walking to a venue – possibly with a laptop bag and in new shoes.

Make a checklist and count items in

To save time and effort working out what you need every time you network, create a checklist (business cards, tablet, phone, charger etc.) and attach it to the inside of your bag to literally count those items in and out. Networking conversations can be scuppered before they even start if you've left one vital piece of cable or a charger at the office or the previous venue and you've no other way to show your products. Forgetting things looks horribly unprofessional and it's stressful too – don't put yourself through it.

Check the weather

Travelling from one end of the country to another to network in one day? Check what the weather will be like where you're going and dress for that, not for where you're leaving from. Temperatures north to south can differ wildly and you can look foolish if your clothing looks inappropriate for the weather outside. Invest in a compact brolly that can be stashed anywhere too – nothing looks worse than wet hair.

Don't be above a dress rehearsal

If this event is really important to you, don't be above doing a dress rehearsal – actually wearing the clothes you plan to wear, actually carrying the laptop bag for two hours, and actually walking from your hotel to the venue to check how long it takes you in new brogues. You may only have to do this a couple of times at the start of your networking 'career'. But it can be time very well spent.

Key take-aways

Write down the things you will take away from Step 1 and how you will implement them.

Topic	Take-away	Implementation
How to identify your existing network	• *Who are the people that I already value, whether close to me or just acquaintances?*	• *Check my address book and Facebook friends.*
How to rediscover your existing network		
How to identify who your real allies are		
Learn ways to gain confidence from your existing network		
How to create new networks		
The appropriate attitude for networking		
Practical preparation for events		
The contents of a business card		
How to plan networking effectively		
Tools that will help shape network planning		
How to become physically prepared for networking events		

Step 2

NETWORK EFFECTIVELY ONLINE

'Let's get real about this.
Connection is what humans crave.'
— *Stephen Fry, Actor, Author, Presenter*
and Social Media Enthusiast

Five ways to succeed

- Check your network's social media updates every day.

- Keep your social media personal profile information up to date.

- Maintain your online brand consistently and with integrity.

- Customize all default social media invites.

- Be mindful of social media law.

Five ways to fail

- Prioritize social media over face to face interaction.

- Use your personal Facebook page to do business networking.

- Post anything, whether business-related or not.

- Respond immediately to upsetting social media activity.

- Never meet social media contacts face to face.

What is online networking?

Networking relies on keeping all your important relationships in a state of health and good repair. It's a time-consuming activity that needs planning and motivation, especially if your network is a growing one. To help manage large networks while still staying in touch, more and more business people are complementing traditional networking methods with the use of social media such as Facebook, Twitter, LinkedIn® and others. Such sites offer simple ways of keeping in regular touch that take up little time and don't cost money. They allow you to update your whole network, or a group within it, with what's new in your world – all in a single action. Such 'push updates' can help keep your contacts to feel valued and up to date.

What are the options?

While there are hordes of social networking sites out there to choose from, three could be said to be the 'big players' – at least at the moment.

Facebook

You may be acquainted with Facebook, so we won't go into any detail. For personal use, Facebook allows you to create your online profile, find and add other users as friends, post photos, send messages and join like-minded groups online. In this arena, its core premise is friendship or shared experience: it's likely you'll know, or at least have met, everyone you add as a friend on Facebook. For professional and business use Facebook is a flexible hub for contact details, product or services information, engaging content and interacting with clients. See www.facebook.com.

LinkedIn®

Presence on LinkedIn® is increasingly seen as a 'must-have' in the world of business. Users create a personal profile including their curriculum vitae, key skills and expertise, detailed work experience and more. Literally designed to extend and enhance the process of networking, registered users can invite anyone with whom they have some level of professional relationship to become a 'connection', effectively providing the user with a database of contacts and their specialist knowledge. Business people use it to stay in touch, stay abreast of the job market, or seek work. Employers use it to list jobs, search for, and check out potential candidates. By showing the user the connections of their connections, LinkedIn® also demonstrates opportunities for introductions through mutual contacts. See www.linkedin.com.

Twitter

Twitter is a social networking service whose core premise is that of 'micro-blogging', where users post and read messages or 'Tweets' of 140 characters or less. To receive Tweets, you must follow people or groups that interest you, whether they be friends, celebrities, brands, columnists, newspapers – or interesting strangers. Tweets are presented in a timeline, creating a concise and immediate digest of what's happening in the world that interests you. Unlike Facebook, there's no assumption that you need to know someone before following them. It is acceptable to follow, say, a celebrity, and open dialogue with them by replying to their Tweets. It is perhaps this lure of instant access to high-profile people that has been central to the ever-increasing popularity of Twitter. If you follow someone and they then choose to follow you, a further layer of communication is offered in the form of 'direct messaging' or the 'DM'. These Tweets are not public, but can be exchanged between two parties who follow each other in addition to default public Tweets. See www.twitter.com.

What are their intended audiences?

LinkedIn® is strictly professional – the work-life you, always at your best; Facebook, though most used for personal updates, is increasingly being harnessed by people to profile their business or profession entirely distinct from their personal Facebook account. Twitter can be used judiciously to post updates that may appeal to both personal and professional contacts – you could think of it as 'first-date you' – the whole story, but at its best.

Making social media work for you

We've identified the options, but what, in real terms, do you 'do' with social media? What functions can they carry out to enhance and extend your face to face networking?

How should I use them?

Looking at some key areas of social media sites will get you started, allowing you to learn more on the way.

- **Review your profile:** On sites where your employment information, work and skills are displayed, such as LinkedIn®, ensure they're correct. Ensure that your profile is complete, proofed, and bang up to date.

- **Check what your contacts are doing:** Your daily routine should include checking what your contacts are doing via their status updates and posts on Facebook, LinkedIn® or Twitter etc. Use this information to help initiate and personalise your contact with them. So, for example, you may congratulate someone within LinkedIn® for their new job status update, or, contrastingly, email a contact after seeing their Tweet about an event they'd attended. Opening with 'Hi, I saw your Tweet about the London event – it sounded great!' gives you an excuse for getting in touch, and shows you're taking long-term interest.

■ **Post regular updates:** Known informally as 'pinging', posting regular updates to LinkedIn®, Twitter and Facebook helps keep you in the front of many people's minds. Share information and articles through these platforms to offer value to your contacts in an efficient manner. Pinging allows others to passively digest what's going on in your life and what your hopes are. From your posts they'll build a picture of your goals and aspirations. If they want to respond, they can and will.

■ **Ask or answer questions:** People like answering a question authoritatively: if you want a reaction from your social media network, ask a question! LinkedIn® has an answers feature where you can both ask and answer questions, giving you the opportunity to demonstrate your curiosity about business and showcase your knowledge to an interested audience.

■ **Post comments or likes:** Make personal contact quickly by commenting on someone's status on Facebook or LinkedIn®. If you are pushed for time, even hitting 'like' or re-Tweeting will bring your name to the front of someone's mind briefly, making them feel good about the fact you noticed.

■ **Endorse:** LinkedIn's® endorsement function allows you to attest to a contact's skills and expertise. Use this feature only to authenticate skills that are proven. By endorsing judiciously, everyone wins. Your contact builds a strong and verified skills profile, you give them a useful and appropriate 'gift', and everyone feels good about the transaction. Most people you endorse will also reciprocate in their own time.

Social media and privacy

Making social media work for, not against you, relies on having a strong awareness at all times of what you want people to see and what you don't.

Facebook and privacy

If you're starting your own business, create a Facebook page for the business itself, entirely removed from your own page on Facebook. Then you can maintain two discrete accounts, promoting your professional image on your business page, while keeping your off-duty presence (and friends) private on your personal account. Keep these parts of your life separate – you don't want clients to see you in a compromising snap. Furthermore, if and when you do create a Facebook account for your business or profession, check that your *personal* account is then private, meaning access to your photos and information is only available to those you've carefully accepted as friends. Bear in mind that some big companies now block the use of Facebook by staff – even remote staff. If Facebook is your main medium for social media business promotion, ensure that companies you hope to work with are keen on using Facebook.

Twitter

Because you will aim to have followers on Twitter who are both personal and professional contacts, be careful what you write. Be positive. Never swear. If you are having a bad day, don't Tweet about it. Negativity and cynicism can be a turn-off, and criticism of others can be dangerous. Read on for more information on social media and the law.

Create the brand of you

What makes a brand? Perhaps an important element is consistency: a strong brand creates clear associations in our minds. Stop anyone in the street and they could probably describe the core values of Coca Cola, Sony or Apple in a few words, and those very words would resemble those chosen by other people. But people are brands too. Consider celebrities: the more successful they are, the more they embody one core persona. You expect them to look and behave in a certain way. We feel comfortable when people are consistent, and harnessing this simple human preference for consistency can be a powerful tool in successful networking. We've seen in the preceding Steps that your face-to-face brand is extremely important, and you've been working hard to develop it. You also need to do the same with your online presence.

To take networking seriously you may have to work on your online brand; the brand that is you. 'Google' yourself on the Internet – it can be an eye opener. This is what a new contact could find if they wanted to do some background research on you. It's up to you to start creating the picture you want to present: professional, positive and consistent.

Building your online brand

Creating an online brand sounds complicated, but it isn't: it's simply the process of ensuring that what people can find about you online is consistent with, and underlines, the persona you've worked hard to develop face to face. It's checking that everything hangs together, and creates a holistic picture of someone trustworthy and professional.

■ **Act on your Google results:** Did you see anything up there that you wouldn't want potential clients to see? If they're within your control, take them down or lock them down to friends only. Negotiate with friends who've posted embarrassing snaps or posts about you. Use your judgement – everyone relaxes on holidays and nights out, so don't become too obsessive. But if you're portrayed breaking the law, bending rules, or playing hookie from work, remove this material.

■ **Think of your social media as a suite:** Scrutinize your LinkedIn® profile and posts, your Tweets, your Facebook activity, and your blog if you have one. Each of these media serve different purposes with different levels of formality, but underneath that, do you hear a core, consistent voice running through them? If not, you may need to spend more time considering how you want to come across, and keep this in the front of your mind every time you post, re-Tweet or upload. We'll look at this in detail next.

■ **Act like you're famous:** When online, it's safest to act as if you have the paparazzi on your tail. Google doesn't forget, or keep secrets.

Create a house style

Used by publishing houses and most big companies, a house style ensures that everything a company writes is presented in a consistent way, no matter who produced it – from CEO to receptionist. House styles are large documents we couldn't reproduce here, but their core premise is standardization. Search the web for 'house style manual' or 'house style guide' and you'll find loads of examples, which you can tweak to suit you. In the meantime start thinking about the following headers:

- **Spelling:** Do you favour UK or American spellings? Dependent on your market you may want to decide between one of these two conventions. Decide, and stick with it – don't mix and match.

- **Capitalization:** Do you write your job title or company name with initial capitals? Perhaps you use initial caps to name the techniques you use or skills you have. Note these and apply them consistently.

- **Presentation:** Do you have a tagline, logo, or other feature that you like to use when you write online? Ensure that you use and place these features in a consistent manner every time they appear.

- **Tone:** it may be helpful for you to list a few words about how you want all of your writing and posts to come across, e.g. 'helpful', 'knowledgeable', 'up to date'. Check every comment or Tweet against this list before you post and you will soon develop a recognizable voice.

Social media etiquette

Even in the virtual world of social media, common sense and courtesy still apply. Consider the following when you're deciding whether to post or not to post.

- **Quantity:** Effective posting relies on balance. Over-post or over-Tweet and people will get bored of you. Post too little and you'll appear absent and uninteresting. Post regularly before networking events; it's discourteous to point people to your social media, for them only to find it empty.

- **Relevance:** Is what you want to say relevant to those following you? It needn't be about business, but does it still offer value or insight to others, or showcase your curiosity about life and learning?

- **Timeliness:** Be prompt in your posting about events. Keep an eye on the news too: you'll cause offence by celebrating a business milestone on the same day as a national disaster. Post a respectful note of sympathy or, even better, fall silent for a day.

- **Appropriateness:** Be sensitive to what may offend, especially when posting to a multi-cultural following. Avoid topics such as religion, alcohol, and the place of women in some societies.

- **Standards:** Spell-check, use your house style and be consistent. Avoid using text-speak to get under 140 characters in Twitter; reword instead.

■ **Personalize default invites:** Many social media sites offer simple 'invite' functions: Facebook and LinkedIn® may be the most familiar to you. While these are helpful features, don't rely on the sterile default message to invite others to your network – it can come across as cold and insincere. Always customize your initial request to new friends and connections with a personal message, reminding them of where you met or what you have in common. We'll look at this in more detail next.

■ **Never post in anger:** Never post in a knee-jerk reaction to something that has upset or angered you. You could destroy your brand, both face to face and online, in seconds with an ill-advised post that you can't take back. If you do feel strongly about something, draft a post or message and sleep on it. The morning will bring better judgement and a fresh perspective.

Sounding Pro: Customized LinkedIn® invitations

On LinkedIn® it's imperative to be professional – especially at your initial approach. Using the default invite is a bit abrupt, and doesn't impress. So, to get this crucial 'first impression moment' right, let's look a little closer at customization. Remember: connecting to someone you've never met can bear fruit, but you should try for a mutual introduction first.

Connecting with someone you have met:

Greet them by name.	*Hello Stella,/Morning Richard,*
In a positive light, remind them where you met.	*It was good to meet you at Tuesday's networking event.*
Ask for permission or state your wish to connect.	*I wonder whether I could add you to my LinkedIn® network?*

Connecting with someone you've never met and may or may not have shared contacts with:

Greet them by name	*Good morning Steven,*
Introduce yourself	*I'm Peter Gregg, director at Delta Marketing.*
Explain how you know of them	*I've been following your blog since it was recommended to me by our shared connection, Charlotte Walsh.*
Explain why you would like to connect	*Since implementing some of your ideas in my business, we've had great results. I'd like to connect with you so that I may keep up to date with you and your work.*

Social media law

Most professional journalists and columnists will have swotted up on media law as part of their training. Contrastingly, the spare-room blogger, poster, or Tweeter may never have given these topics a second's thought. But the numbers are sobering; more than 650 people in England and Wales faced criminal charges in 2012 for comments they posted on Facebook or Twitter alone. If you want to make safe use of social media, best do your homework.

Libel

Libel is 'a published false statement that is damaging to a person's reputation, or a written defamation'. The law is clear that if you write a post or Tweet like this, it is as serious as publishing it in a newspaper (and that goes for re-Tweeting too). Recent court cases have seen public figures begin to seek libel damages from large numbers of social media users over false accusations and even insinuations. Never post, forward or re-Tweet anything that could damage another person's reputation – you can't be jailed but could land yourself a damages bill, and lose all professional credibility into the bargain.

Copyright

Written copy, photos and other media (e.g. video clips) are all subject to UK copyright law, even on social media. So you cannot use them without the express permission of the owner, who is within their rights to expect payment or at least be credited for the work. Passing off someone else's work as your own via a social media platform is copyright infringement; not only is it a criminal offence, it will also break the policies of the media site you are using, with serial offenders potentially being suspended or blocked. There are loopholes for using 'orphan' items whose copyright owner cannot be traced, either because the item is very old and may no longer be in copyright or because widespread use makes the true origin of the item difficult to trace or prove. But err on the side of caution – don't assume that a 'group misuse' of an item will cover you against the law or the true copyright holder. Copyright infringement can result in a short sentence, a fine, or both.

As an active networker you may be creating your own original work or 'intellectual property' and have posted these or forwarded them to valued contacts. If you then find that your copyright is infringed by someone via social media, the best approach is to contact that person first: ask them to remove the content or at least credit you. If you don't get results, raise the infringement issue with the site itself, and they can take action for you.

Threats

Avoid posting anything that could be construed as a threat – some social media users have got themselves into real hot water by making such idle threats unthinkingly. The 2003 Communications Act states that it is an offence to send a 'menacing electronic communication', even if you don't really mean it. In an attempt to protect freedom of speech in social media, there has been some fine-tuning of the criteria for prosecution under this Act. However, if the threat seems credible, or exhibits racism or other prejudices, or is part of a wider harassment, the verdict will still be a jail sentence.

Offensive comments

Mind your manners on social media. Posting comments that could cause serious offence or expressing very strong views that may upset some groups can land social media users with a jail sentence. As more and more cases of this kind have been coming to court, again there has been some fine-tuning to protect freedom of speech – a basic human right as set down by the European Convention. However, the criteria for this offence is fairly subjective, and can rely on how the prosecuting body interprets the law.

The law is having to adapt quickly to keep up with social media, both to protect people from abuses and to protect their basic human rights to free speech. If you are serious about using social media in your networking activities then it's in your interests to stay abreast of the law. See www.lawsociety.org.uk and www.socialmediaexaminer.com.

Integrating your activity

Here are a few suggestions to make social media work even better for you:

■ Tell contacts where to find you

If you're on Facebook, Twitter and LinkedIn®, you may feel that you're jumping from one to another to contact a discreet audience in each. You can better reach your audience by encouraging them across to other additional (appropriate) platforms. Ensure your email signature carries your web address and prompts to follow you on, Twitter your business Facebook page etc. Adding the small interactive media icons makes it easier for others to engage with you too.

■ **Tempt your contacts across media**

Written a great article? Post it on your website, but Tweet its location to your Twitter followers, post it on your Facebook page, but mention the location on LinkedIn®, and vice versa across your media. Regularly drawing your contacts into watching you and interacting with you across platforms can both give them a fuller picture of your activities and lessen the load for you.

■ **Exhibit your social media posts on your website**

If it's appropriate, Twitter feeds, Facebook posts and similar can be incorporated into a portion of your website, bringing the real-time activity of social media onto the more static platform of a website. This can encourage previously website and email-based contacts to learn what you're doing in a more immediate way, and ultimately to follow you on other platforms.

■ **Consider using a social media management system**

If you use several social media sites it can be a challenge to keep up with what your network community is saying, and with what you are saying in each platform too. Clever toolkits such as Hootsuite, Tweetreach, Social Bakers (and many more) can pull all of your social media together to help you create, and digest, more activity in the manner most convenient to you, while keeping the experience unchanged for your contacts. You'll need to do some research to find the best fit for you.

Getting back round the table

While social media offer near-effortless ways of speaking to a large number of people at a time, they do, as a by-product, create busy routes of networking traffic, vying for our attentions. Users may sometimes feel overwhelmed by the volume of virtual contact and information they receive. We should remind ourselves that networking is about human relationships and human partnerships first and foremost, and nothing can replace the simple act of talking face to face.

Ensure that you always come back to table: make time to meet your contacts regularly, to shake hands, have coffee and laugh. Sharing ideas face to face is networking gold. And strive for simplicity; turn your phone off, leave the iPad in the office and concentrate wholly on the person you are with.

Don't assume that a contact who seems to thrive on social media is content to stay there: meet them. If another hangs back, uncomfortable with the technology, do the same: meet them. At its simplest, networking is simply the act of getting on with people. We should always strive to cut through the hi-tech distraction to get back to the clarity of talking, and – more importantly – listening. It's where it all starts.

Key take-aways

Write down the things you will take away from Step 2 and how you will implement them.

Topic	Take-away	Implementation
What the options are for social media networking	• *Three main players at present: Facebook, LinkedIn® and Twitter*	• *Think about registering on LinkedIn®*
How to use the different social media appropriately		
How to make social media work for me in my networking		
Social media and privacy		
How to identify my online brand		
How to build my online brand through integrity and consistency		
Social media etiquette		
Customizing default social media invites		
Social media law		
How to integrate my social media activity		
Getting my contacts back round a table		

SECURE AN INVITATION

*'You never get a second chance
to make a first impression.' Anon.*

Five ways to succeed

- Networking isn't scary; it's just meeting new people.
- Arrive early at events.
- Bring business cards.
- Prepare something short to say about yourself.
- Smile!

Five ways to fail

- Hang out with people you know.
- Dismiss new people that aren't 'important' enough.
- Wait for others to approach you.
- Hog the conversation.
- Try to 'get' something from everyone you meet.

Invitations

You may receive invitations to networking events by post, by email, through LinkedIn® or even by text. Here's what to do when you get an invite.

Prioritize: make events work for you, not against you

You might work in a business area that attracts interest from event organizers. You might be getting 'encouragement' from your manager to get out there more. This is good, but neither your diary nor your workload will allow you to network all the time: you must prioritize. Only choose events that may have valuable relevance to you, and that work with your diary.

What's the field?: research your hosts

Not sure whether the event will provide any real opportunities? Research the hosts, of whom there may be several. Take ten minutes to look them up online, get a little company history and find out their field of business. Five minutes on the web will give you enough information to decide whether or not to invest the time in attending. On the other hand, if you are networking to take a career sidestep or to break into new markets, networking at an event not directly placed in your business area could reap some useful new contacts.

RSVPs: avoid a faux pas

Different invites expect different responses from you. While this area of networking will always change with the development of new media, some basic guidelines still hold true.

■ **For invites by post:** If the event hosts require a firm RSVP from you, then the invite will offer contact details for getting in touch by phone, email, or other means. In cases like this you should definitely RSVP by the date given or you may lose your place. Some invites may say 'regrets only', in which case they only want to hear from you if you can't make it. You should assume that you will be attending alone, unless the invite explicitly states otherwise.

■ **By email:** Email is the new 'post'; it behaves much the same way, and demands similar etiquette. If a networking invitation email is emailed specifically to you, it likely requires an RSVP. If there is no mention of one, it's still sensible to send one. For email, it is always safest to err on the side of courtesy; it is, addressed specifically to you after all, and bears all the weight of a formal invitation.

■ **By Facebook or LinkedIn®:** You may receive quite frequent invites through both Facebook and LinkedIn®, and yet there are no hard and fast etiquette rules in these media. While many people ignore such group invites to events, it's still courteous to RSVP. A courteous reply may just get you remembered a second time. And frankly, if you are really serious about networking, any excuse to use your or your company's name is good publicity. It only takes a couple of seconds to respond with a decline or accept. Do remember to follow through on what you have said, however.

■ **Twitter:** Unless you've had a direct message (often referred to simply as a 'DM') from the event hosts, you can safely assume that any invites to networking events are just open Tweets and neither need nor expect a response from you. Keep an eye on your timeline though, to see if any interesting names reply to the Tweet, which may influence your decision to attend.

In all cases, once you have responded to an invitation, do follow through with what you have promised. The basic human courtesies that apply to social situations also apply to business. It's not acceptable to say you will be there and back out on the day – even if it's because of valid work pressures. Nor should you compromise by sending someone in your place. It's common practice for attendees to request a delegate list in order to do their homework and plan an effective morning's networking. At the very least, most people will scan the name-tags at the front door to give themselves a layout of who they would like to meet first. By not turning up, your unexplained absence might just sour a fledgling business relationship or scupper the deal of a lifetime. You never know who was all psyched up to meet you that day.

Get advance intelligence: Find out who's going

If there was ever one 'top tip' for networking preparation, it is this: *find out who is going.* The mere fact of knowing who will be there gives you an incredibly strong advantage. If you RSVP by phone or email, ask the organizers to send you a list of delegates – they will be used to that request. That way, you'll see the names of those attending and where they work, and you can do your homework. Some extra prep now can make life easier on the day. Pick out the people on the list that you really want to meet and do some research. Find a photo of them and get a little background information. Introducing yourself to a potential client is a whole lot more graceful when you can pick out their face from a distance rather than having to squint embarrassingly at a series of chest-height name tags. Check the rest of the list for people you already know who might be able to introduce you to your goal contact, rather than having to do it yourself. If you are nervous, the delegate list is your particular friend. Look for one or two names you already know amongst the attendees. This will give you a familiar face to seek out in the first ten, nervy minutes while you settle in, and someone who can provide a breather between more demanding introductions. Pepper the event with (brief) respites like this and you'll be fine.

Dress, body language and attitude

Many successful business people swear blind that there is no substitute for meeting face to face. Why? Possibly because it's visual, honest and upfront – this is the real you standing here meeting people, so make it the best 'you' you've got.

Dress

It's not rocket science to suggest that when meeting new people, it's a good idea to look your best. However, networking events can take place at any number of venues outside of the office and office hours, leaving you wondering whether business attire is still appropriate.

- **Don't overdress:** Networking is not an interview, it's a chance to meet new people, and you don't want to look desperate by overdressing. If you are unsure about what to wear, ask others who are attending. That way, you won't turn up clutching your briefcase, in a brand-new suit and tie, when everyone else is relaxing in business casual. For unusual venues, weekend or evening events, it's less likely that business attire is expected. In instances like these, a call to the organizers wouldn't go amiss – you won't be the only one checking either. If you're still in doubt, business casual is always a safe default position.

■ **Avoid clothes that make you fidget:** At all costs, avoid cloth-ing that needs constant adjustment. Choose clothing that stays where it is put and looks good while it's at it. Fiddling with your clothing could be misconstrued for nerves, will impact on your self-confidence, and will distract you and the people you meet from the job in hand. Public figures who are good in front of a camera are sure and 'large' in action, rarely making small, tense, fidgety movements.

■ **Be comfortable:** If there is ever any one rule about clothes, it's this: don't wear something uncomfortable no matter how great it looks. It's obvious when someone is ill at ease in their clothes or shoes. If you are visibly uncomfortable you'll not feel your best, nor come across as confidently as you might want. Go for clothes and shoes that make you *feel* as well as look good, that don't crush too easily (like linen for example) that you walk well in, and that you can happily stand in for long periods.

■ **Be presentable:** No matter what the time or venue, basic rules apply – never look dishevelled, even if you have just made a long journey. Everything you wear should be clean and ironed. Shoes should be super-clean. And check your teeth too.

■ **Use the cloakroom:** Get rid of excess luggage and overcoats and enter unencumbered. Pare down what you carry to the essentials so that you can have free hands to meet and greet easily.

Body language and your positive attitude

Research suggests that people start forming their first impressions of you within seconds, and that over 50 per cent of communication is non-verbal. If the research is true, it means you'll have to cut a positive figure from the moment you walk in the door, and watch your body language until you step back through it.

- **Walk in with purpose:** Walk decisively through the door, and do your best to look happy. Scan the room for faces you recognize or displays that catch your interest. Feign purpose, even if you don't have it. Seasoned networkers may even pause at the door to look around – it breathes confidence and lets everyone who might want to meet you know that you have arrived. It takes guts, but gives you a great vantage point of the room and where you want to aim first before you 'commit' to your first steps. A word to the wise about your 'entrance': if you wear glasses normally, don't think that you will cut a better figure without them at a networking event. Wear them, or invest in contacts – screwing up your eyes to find people and read displays is not a good look, and it ruins your body language. Try standing tall when you can't see a metre ahead of you. Not easy. By going in short-sighted, you will also be removing all possibility of those chance (and lucky) meetings you weren't expecting – you quite simply won't spot them as they walk on by.

■ **Watch your habits:** Do you have a telltale nervous habit that's an unfortunate window on your soul? Many of us touch our noses, pull at our ears, play with our hair, cross our arms defensively, or talk through our fingers when we feel out of our depth. Ask a trusted friend if you have a giveaway tic like this, identify it, and learn to resist it. Nervous habits speak volumes we really don't want to say when networking.

■ **Shake hands like you mean it:** When introducing yourself to someone, offer a short, purposeful handshake: a limp one can suggest you're not interested in the other person at all. A handshake is central to positive first impressions, and that first moment of contact – of 'touch' in real terms – can say an awful lot about you very quickly.

■ **Make eye contact and smile:** Far from groundbreaking stuff, but when you are meeting someone for the first time, make eye contact with them and smile. Confident eye contact tells people that you are interested in them, that you are a good listener, and that you value what they have to say. Eye contact builds trust, makes a great first impression and leaves a lasting one. Smiling is understood in all countries and across all cultures. It builds trust and makes everyone relax. The simple act of smiling triggers the brain to release endorphins, the 'feel-good' hormone, so you're doing yourself a favour too.

■ **Don't prolong the agony:** Don't spend too much time scanning the room and pointedly reading displays – you are just putting off the inevitable. Introduce yourself to someone fairly promptly. It doesn't matter if your first attempts don't go brilliantly – you are just getting a feel for the crowd. This phase of 'integrating' into the event is a visually important one: people will note that you are moving around well and seem easy to talk to. If, on the other hand, you hover around and fail to introduce yourself, it's likely you will soon start to look shifty after a while. You'll seem less approachable and introductions will be harder.

■ **Expect nothing:** When people think about networking their minds conjure up images of fast-dealing, cut-throat business people trying to squeeze what they want out of others over a lunch date. The reality is far from that, and networking events are (in the main) somewhat gentler affairs. Don't expect to 'get' anything from networking events to begin with, other than a few business cards and also some knowledge about your industry. Don't aim for some kind of 'result' by the time you pick up your coat to leave. Instead, invest your time in initiating conversations with, and genuinely listening to, other people. Even if you don't get to talk much about yourself, your attentiveness will make a lasting impression. Networking is a slow process that only starts to reap rewards over time. Be patient.

Meeting and greeting – what to do

How to introduce yourself

We all know what an introduction is – you make yourself known to someone by shaking hands, and giving your name with a little information about yourself. In a networking situation you are likely to give a little more (business) information than you might offer in a social context. But what and how much information should you give? The following items of information are an appropriate start.

1 name
2 job title
3 company
4 company location
5 why you are here

It's still good practice to say 'Good morning' or 'Good afternoon', or the less formal 'Hello' rather than 'Hi' when you are first meeting someone in a business context. If you are a person who forgets names easily, it might be helpful to repeat the names you learn as you respond to an introduction: 'Ah, Richard, pleased to meet you too.' This will help commit the name to memory, as well as making the other person feel good.

Remember, too, to 'ask permission' to introduce yourself if you are making the first approach: 'Do you mind if I introduce myself?' and 'I hope I'm not interrupting, but I'm …' . Courtesy: it's what networking thrives on.

The elevator pitch

The 'elevator pitch' is an imagined scenario used the world over by business people, life coaches and motivational speakers to prepare us for that million-dollar question 'What do you do?' Imagine you are in the elevator of an office you are visiting. You realize someone you have been desperate to meet and possibly do business with is standing next to you. You've suddenly got a 20- to 30-second golden opportunity to introduce yourself and make such a positive impression that they'll want to continue the conversation beyond that elevator ride. What would you say? Have a think then read the following.

Key pointers

Making a good first impression is an important skill but many people don't do it very well. They get nervous, mixed up, or forgetful, often missing out the most important information. So what do you need to say? Remember five things:

1 **Your name:** say your name clearly.

2 **Your job:** say what your job title is, or if it's more informative, simply what you do.

3 **Company:** say what company you work for.

4 **Location:** say where the company is.

5 **Your elevator pitch:** give a short summary about you (or your company), what you do, and what benefits you bring that you make you unique.

Creating an elevator pitch

So, your elevator pitch says something about you (or your company) but crucially also sells a perceived 'benefit' to a potential client and describes what makes that unique. Remember your elevator pitch is designed just to whet the appetite of the person you're pitching to – to get them asking you for more information and get the two of you talking. It may take several tries to get your elevator pitch right. Here are some useful dos and don'ts:

Do

■ Keep it simple.

■ Be short and to the point.

■ Try to keep a conversational tone of voice.

■ Practise delivering it out loud before an event: you will soon find out if it's too long or sounds awkward – if you get out of breath it's not right.

■ Focus on the benefits you offer clients, don't focus on yourself.

■ Relax and smile when you get the chance to deliver your elevator pitch.

Don't

■ Rush to cram bags of information into 20 seconds (think of those awful radio ads that try to read out terms and conditions in three seconds flat).

■ Use business jargon or acronyms.

■ Exaggerate.

■ Sound over-rehearsed.

■ Tell them everything.

Sounding Pro

Let's take all those jigsaw pieces and put them together. We should now have a fair idea of what you might sound like when it's time to introduce yourself.

Asking permission	Do you mind if I introduce myself?
	I hope I'm not interrupting, but my name is [*your name*].
Saying hello	Good morning, I'm [*your name*].
	Hello, my name's [*your name*].
Saying what your job is	I'm a project manager.
	I'm the creator of a new eco-friendly packaging range.
Saying where you work	I work for Life Screen, an online advertising agency.
	I'm self-employed.
Giving the company's location	The company's based in Surrey.
	I'm based in Southampton.
Making your elevator pitch	Life Screen specializes in interactive online advertising. Our ads are designed to increase brand awareness by 55 per cent in three months. We're testing new technologies all the time to ensure that our clients' ads stay ahead of the rest. Over the next 18 months we're aiming to expand into Europe by investing in partner agencies in France.

Deal with networking nerves

It's good to have a few comforting thoughts before a networking event:

■ You're only in this room for a couple of hours.

■ If you mess up, you may never see most of these people again.

■ Every single person in this room feels EXACTLY the same as you.

1 Don't plan to fail

If you obsess about things going wrong, then they very likely will. So, do the opposite. Instead of dreading a networking event, see the positives. 'I'll get to meet some new people, I'm going to enjoy it'. In the days before an event, imagine yourself there, getting on fine, conversing, and exchanging business cards. Plan to have a good time!

2 Don't be late

By arriving later, you are making things harder for yourself. When a networking event is in full swing, delegates have already begun to make their introductions and are more likely to be engaged in conversations in small groups. These will look and feel pretty hard to join when you are on the outside looking in. Arrive early and many people will still be moving freely around the room, making it much easier to strike up a conversation or introduce yourself.

3 Set (very) manageable targets

To help you through the event successfully, and to make it bearable while you're at it, set some immediate goals; yours. And they have to be concrete. Abstract goals like 'I have to make a great impression' are not going to help. You're more likely to work yourself into more of a lather wondering whether you've made a 'great impression' yet. Instead set yourself tangible targets that you *can* achieve and that will give you a satisfying sense of completion. These could be anything from 'I'm going to introduce myself to three completely new people', to 'I'll collect eight business cards to follow up'. When you've met your goal, relax, and hit the nibbles: job done. You'll probably then find that you'll go on to do your best networking after that moment – without even thinking about it.

4 Cut a deal with yourself

If you are one of those people who finds networking events difficult no matter how you approach them, then be realistic and give yourself the reassurance of an agreed exit point. Don't, however, promise yourself that you can leave at a certain time – you'll just watch the clock and achieve little else. Instead, take a set number of business cards, say, ten, and allow yourself to cut and run only when you've handed them all out. That way, even if you didn't manage anything else, there are at least ten people on the planet who now have your contact details. It's a good start, honest.

5 Smile

It sounds naff and clichéd, I know, but it works. Even if you feel miserably nervous, don't look it. A ready, responsive smile (rather than a fixed grimace) is at once engaging and relaxing. It relaxes you and the person with whom you're about to strike up a conversation, smoothing the way for everyone to talk more easily. Back up your smile with some quiet positive thinking too: in those moments between introductions let your mind wander around good things – the approaching weekend, the prospect of a kip on the train home, anything of comfort. It will visibly free up the tension from your face and your body language, making you easier for others to approach.

6 It's not all about you

If you feel like a rabbit caught in headlights, then hop out of the headlights. Turn the focus away from yourself and take interest in your fellow man. Ask questions, get others talking about themselves; whether it's about their business or something they care passionately about. You can step back for a moment to draw breath, while they can have the pleasure of talking about what interests them most. Even if business gets left behind and you don't get your pitch across, they'll likely remember your name, and that you're engaging, perceptive and a good listener to boot – pretty decent attributes in business, I'll say.

7 Get networking in perspective

Networking is about meeting people who might be useful to you. It's not about 'doing' the business that pays your mortgage. You don't have to get anything done in this couple of hours: you don't have to make any tough negotiations or cut deals. You're simply here to collect a set of acquaintances who might come in handy at some point, and to make a lasting impression on them. Remember to take the hard stuff 'offline'; just chat, collect business cards and try to come across well. The difficult transactions, the 'buy/sell' will come much later. So, for now, chill out.

Key take-aways

Write down the things you will take away from Step 3 and how you will implement them.

Topic	Take-away	Implementation
How to prioritize networking events	• *Ensure it's in my field.* • *Ensure I have enough time to enjoy and benefit from it.*	• *Do more web research when I get invites.* • *Make sure I diarize events alongside my project schedules.*
How to respond to invitations		
How to research attending delegates		
How to dress appropriately		
How to manage your body language		
How to introduce yourself		
How to create an elevator pitch		
How to deliver an elevator pitch		
How to cope with nerves		

Step 4

BE THE BEST CONVERSATIONALIST

'Most people do not listen with the intent to understand; they listen with the intent to reply.'
— Stephen R. Covey, Author

Five ways to succeed

- Encourage others to talk more than you.
- Use open questions without revealing your opinions.
- Take time for courtesy in all business networking.
- Find out how your voice sounds to others.
- Ease conversation with approachable body language.

Five ways to fail

- Don't concentrate on what the other person says.
- Ensure that you get your opinions across.
- Ignore body language and tone of voice.
- Always get straight to the point.
- Don't make eye contact.

Active Listening

To be the best conversationalist, you need to be the best listener. Take this quiz to find out what kind of listener you are.

Which of the following statements sound like you?

1 It is difficult to start a conversation with people I don't know. ☐

2 I like meeting new people. I walk up and say hello. ☐

3 I prefer to stick around people I know and like. ☐

4 I don't talk to people I don't know until I'm introduced. ☐

5 I often talk too much when I meet new people. ☐

6 I interrupt people when they are talking. ☐

7 I get impatient if I have to listen for a long time. ☐

8 I judge what people say, and if I don't like it I interrupt. ☐

9 I am happy to listen and not talk. ☐

10 I don't interrupt and I pause before I reply. ☐

If you've answered yes to statements 1, 3, 4 or 5, you might need help building your confidence for meeting new people. If you've answered yes to 2, 6, 7 or 8, then you may need to work on your listening skills so you get more out of conversation. If you answered yes to 9 or 10, then you're doing well!

Remember: the secret of successful networking is to be a good listener.

Research has identified four types of listener:

Non-listeners

Non-listeners are more interested in what they have to say themselves than in the person they are talking to. They hog conversations, talk all the time, and may be 'space invaders' who use their overbearing physical proximity to push a point. They have a lot to say and they say it. They may fill in the natural gaps in their own monologue using long 'ums' and 'ems' so that no one else gets the chance to step into the conversation. They will actively talk over others who attempt to interject, and will even talk over other people's 'verbal nods' such as 'really?' and 'oh, I see' and 'I couldn't agree more'. They will leave a conversation having remembered little or anything other people managed to squeeze in, and will invariably have the last word.

Marginal listeners

Marginal listeners are also more interested in what they have to say themselves than the person they are talking to. But they hijack what the other person says as a way of getting round to what they want to talk about. They often interrupt so that they can tell you what they think about what you are talking about. Marginal listeners often get impatient. They may show this by finishing other people's sentences, making restless eye moments, finger tapping, or shuffling their feet around. They will frequently check their phones for texts, emails and messages, and are easily distracted by things going on around them.

Pretend listeners

Pretend listeners appear to listen but are actually observing other people's characters and judging what they say. As they listen, they are deciding how to respond, so they're planning, rather than listening. Pretend listeners are concerned with *what* others say, not with how they feel. Interested only in the content of words, they ignore intonation, body language or facial expression. They're keen on stats, logic and definitions. They will leave a conversation with all the facts, but will be emotionally unaffected.

Active listeners

Active listeners are quiet and sympathetic. They listen to what others say, and pay attention to how they feel by trying to put themselves in their shoes. They encourage people to fully express themselves and to continue speaking. They don't interrupt. They wait for others to finish before they respond. They ask meaningful, neutral questions to allow speakers to develop their own train of thought and conversation, encouraging the speaker onwards without expressing any opinions whatsoever. Active listeners make confident, engaged eye contact, quiet 'verbal nods' like 'I see …' and will support the speaker with facial expressions that underpin key points in the conversation. They will appear 'still', and may lean forward a little to listen. They notice those tiny verbal and visual cues that tell them someone wants to speak, and will 'give the floor' without hesitation. Active listeners respect privacy, personal space, and spot physical barriers – they make take off their specs, remove small obstacles between speakers, or indicate a better place to talk.

The truth is, we are probably all four types of listener at different times, depending on the conversation, how we feel, and who we are with. But becoming a truly active listener can bring huge benefits, and not just when you are networking. People who listen well gain the trust of others far more quickly than poor listeners. Listening fully to others also makes them feel valued. And ironically, we all tend to remember good listeners as fascinating people that we'd like to spend more time with – even though they may not have said very much! Put together, being a good listener helps others think of you as trustworthy, caring and interesting – three vital elements in successful networking.

Active listening using FACE

Some people are 'born listeners' and have an inbuilt aptitude for giving themselves completely to a conversation. These are active listeners. Perhaps you know a few. As people go, they are instantly likeable aren't they? We subconsciously seek out good listeners because they make us feel valued, they help us work out our own thoughts, and because they come across as warm and fascinating people – even though they may not say a lot. Well, the good news is, any one of us can become an active listener, using a technique called FACE. FACE stands for:

- **Focus:** Focus means you focus on the speaker and on nothing else. You ignore incidental noise. You focus not only on the words the speaker says but also on how the speaker feels. You try to appreciate the full experience of the communication without judging what they are saying. The tiniest utterance like 'Hm' or 'Uh huh' can reassure the speaker that you are fully focused on them, as does engaged eye contact, a slight inclination of your head towards the speaker, or facial expressions that reflect back the tone of the conversation (e.g., smiling when talking of successes, concern when the subject is negative).

- **Acknowledge:** This means you recognize both the person's desire to speak and that 'they have the floor'. You may move your head to show that you're listening, or assume facial expressions that mirror the tone of the subject under discussion. Short, unobtrusive expressions like 'I see', 'I understand', show that you're paying attention and support a speaker's unfolding monologue. You may also consider the setting of your conversation – do you want to move away from a noisy area?

- **Clarify:** This means asking simple, meaningful questions to encourage the speaker. Avoid questions that can be answered with a simple 'yes/no' answer, because these can close down a promising conversation prematurely. Open questions encourage fuller responses and allow the conversation to develop onwards. You might ask things like 'What changed your mind?', or 'How did that make you feel?'

- **Empathize:** This means showing that you appreciate the speaker's opinion or experience. You empathize not only through the words you say, but by the tone and volume of your voice, by your body language and appropriate facial expressions. You wouldn't, for example, check your watch when someone was talking about a period of stress at work – you'd assume a concerned expression and nod sympathetically.

When you use the simple basics of FACE, you will find that many people respond better to you, that conversations become more meaningful, and that you are more likely to build better relationships with people you are meeting for the first time.

Sounding Pro: Being an active listener

In reality, what would FACE 'sound' like?

Focus

Focus is largely silent. You do this with non-linguistic gestures, like confident eye contact, inclining your head towards the speaker, maybe holding your chin with your hand. You might utter the occasional 'uh-huh'. You ignore everything around you and concentrate on the speaker. Your body becomes more still.

Acknowledge

I see./I'm with you./Yes, of course.

That's true./Really?/Right!

That's interesting/impressive/surprising.

Clarify

The *wh*– words (*what, when, where, who* and *why* and, by association, *how*) are particularly useful here, as they automatically create open questions that encourage the speaker into a fuller answer without expressing any of your own opinions.

What did you do next?/How did you feel about that?

What would you like to happen now?

How has that affected you?/When was this?

Why do you think that happened?

But there are of course, many ways of asking an open question:

Tell me a bit more about that.

Could you explain that in a little more detail?

Empathize

Great!/How wonderful!/How awful!/Well done!

You must have been relieved./You must be delighted.

Sounding Pro: Follow-up letters and emails

To follow up with a poorly written email or letter could undo the good work you have achieved through face-to-face networking.

Here are seven rules of polite writing and the language that might accompany them.

1	**Greeting politely**	*Dear Anil/Hi Anil* (not just 'Anil')
2	**Thanking for any previous contact and/or open with a friendly statement**	*Thank you for your email/letter.* *I hope you are well.*
3	**Saying you're happy to be in contact**	*Nice to hear from you.* (if you are replying to someone who hasn't written for a long time, or is making first contact).
4	**Congratulating on any successes**	*Congratulations on your promotion.*
5	**Asking politely (don't order people)**	*Could I ask you a favour?* *I wonder whether you could send me … ?*
6	**Saying thank you**	*Thank you very much.* *Thank you in advance.*
7	**Signing off politely**	*Yours faithfully* (very formal) *Yours sincerely* (formal) *Best wishes* (friendly)

By cushioning your business writing with politeness, you are likely to give a positive impression, make the reader feel good, and ultimately get the response you need.

Get to know Jo

What about really getting to know your new colleagues and contacts? Let's move on to conversation in the business environment.

Key pointers

It's important to get to know people personally, as it's the cornerstone to building good relationships. Getting to know colleagues will usually happen in the moments in between the formal schedule of the work day – at the coffee machine, at lunch, in the few minutes before and after meetings, or on business travel.

What you talk about is important – business brings together people from all corners of the globe, and from all cultures too. What may be friendly small talk to one person may feel pretty personal to another. A good way to start conversations on safe and professional territory is to recognize that everyone has different areas of experience; these influence who they are and how they 'tick'. Take the following five areas of experience:

- **National experience** – the country they come from (if it is different from yours)

- **Regional experience** – the area of that country they come from

- **Professional experience** – the work they have done and where they have worked

- **Social experience** – their experience of working in different organizations

- **Personal experience** – their education and travel

You want to know more about a person who is new to your business environment but you want to go about it in a professional, neutral way. 'Get to know Jo' is an exercise to help you find out about the people you meet without risk of over-familiarity or offence. There are five simple questions. If you ask them and follow up with others, you'll be well (and safely) on your way to getting to know your new colleague or contact better.

■ **National experience** – *Where are you from? Do you mind me asking where you are from?*

■ **Regional experience** – *What part of (country) are you from? What's it like there?*

■ **Professional experience** – *When did you start work here? Where did you work before you came here? What did you do before you came here?*

■ **Social experience** – *How different is it working here? How much of a change is this role for you?*

■ **Personal experience** – *Where did you study? Have you any holiday/travel plans this summer? Do you travel a lot with work?*

The responses you get will give you the chance to ask follow-up questions and learn a little more, while staying safely on nationality, region, work and travel. For some people and some cultures, areas like family and social background are just a little too personal to talk about – at least initially.

Voice and vocabulary

Many of us never think twice about the way we speak or how we sound. However, your voice and vocabulary are incredibly important assets in networking and can strongly influence the impression people form of you. Ask yourself the following questions:

■ Do others often ask you to repeat yourself?

■ Do others often ask you to explain something you have said?

■ Do other people turn round to glance at you when I speak?

■ Do you sometimes fall over your words?

■ Do other people sometimes tell you 'not to be so negative'?

If you find that you are answering 'yes' to more than a couple of the questions above, it may be the right time to consider your voice and how you use it. It's no secret that politicians work on their voice quality, pace and delivery to compelling effect. People make assumptions about us (however wrongly) judged on the way we speak. If you are really serious about successful networking, you might want to set aside a little time to fine-tune one of your most persuasive instruments – your voice. Your time will not be wasted.

Ask a friend or colleague to take a video of you speaking. This can be in any setting. Listen and watch for the following:

Pace: do you get out of breath when you speak? If so, it's likely you are speaking far too fast and much of what you say will be missed by those listening to you. Speaking too fast can also suggest nerves or being a bit desperate to keep others in conversation – neither of which are particularly desirable.

Volume: When you're eating out with friends do people look at your table when you first speak? Time to turn down your volume. Talking too loudly suggests overconfidence. At best, it embarrasses people. At worst, they feel bullied. Conversely, if you go through life constantly repeating yourself, it's time to speak up. You have as much right to 'air-time' as the next person, so make yourself heard!

Language: While we won't insult your intelligence by asking you not to swear, beware of other vocabulary that can be just as much of a turn off. Don't use jargon or obscure acronyms to sound impressive, or worse, to put others on the back foot. Similarly, negative language can wear people down. Don't say 'you saved my life there' when 'that was helpful' will do. Try 'challenge' instead of 'disaster', and when someone asks how you are say 'Good! You?' instead of 'Not bad, thanks.' You'll feel happier and so will they.

Body Language

Or as we like to call it: how to act confidently in conversation even when you aren't. It is very important to convey a positive first impression. But how do you sustain that positive impression while in prolonged conversation, especially if you are not feeling confident?

Start every conversation with a handshake

Have you ever noticed how awkward you feel if you are introduced to someone and they make no move to offer a handshake? A handshake jumpstarts the conversation into life with a clear opening, gives you a reason to smile, permission to actually touch the new person you are meeting, and gives you the concrete moment at which you say your name. Conversation started. Simple.

But what makes a good handshake? When you offer a handshake, be sure to extend your whole arm. This tells the other person that you're genuinely happy to meet them. This large movement also frees up tense muscles and helps you feel more confident. Extending your hand weakly from the elbow suggests you're shaking hands reluctantly – this tight, indecisive movement will not help your body relax either.

Your hands speak volumes

So what about grip? We've all experienced the vice-like grip and the 'limp fingertip'. The trick is to find something in between that feels genuine yet comfortable for both parties. Practise on your friends and family first to get it right. Avoid two-handed grips or a secondary elbow-hold until you feel very comfortable with someone.

Orientation is also important. Offer your hand with your thumb facing upwards – a palm facing downwards may suggest that you feel superior or want to control the other. If you get a hand-shake like this, level the playing field by tilting your hands back to vertical. It will boost your self-assurance and send out discreet 'confidence signals' to the person you've just met.

And if you suffer from clammy palms, stash a handkerchief somewhere accessible. When you anticipate an introduction, wipe your hands out of sight. Extending a clean, dry hand will give you confidence.

Stand tall, feel confident

If you want to *feel* confident and fully engaged in conversation, then it's no surprise that the first thing you have to do is *look* confident and fully engaged. As you shake hands with someone new, prepare for sustained conversation by rolling your shoulders back a little. This will straighten your posture, lengthen your spine and make you look taller. You're opening up your lungs too, helping you avoid the curse of the 'shaky voice'. Allow no barriers to creep in between you and the person you are speaking to, so keep your hands out of your pockets, resist folding your arms, and remember not to cross your ankles as you stand either. Standing with an open aspect from head to toe will make you appear more approachable, while allowing you also to breathe properly and stand comfortably. If you feel too upright, loosen up your posture by shifting your weight onto one leg. If you feel exposed or need something in your hands, by all means carry some papers, a glass, or a plate from the buffet. Make sure, however, that you don't use these as props to hide behind – hold them at waist level or below; keep them away from your torso and face.

Achieve the right eye contact

It's important to make eye contact when you are conversing, and it's one skill you must master if you are going to become a fully 'active listener'. Avoiding eye contact sends out very strong messages to the person that you are speaking with that you don't want to speak to them, that you feel inferior, that you lack confidence, or (worse still) all three at once. It makes both 'the avoider' and 'the avoided' feel edgy – and it's catching, resulting in the two of you desperately avoiding eye contact in an ever more tense conversation doomed to failure. An exchange like that would affect anyone's confidence, so take a breath, break the cycle, and meet those eyes! If you find this very difficult, concentrate instead on every word the other person is saying. Forget about your eyes. In time, you will fall naturally into attentive eye contact, and the other person will reciprocate, making both of you feel more confident. Go with your instincts; when it feels natural to break eye contact for a second, it probably is the right time – don't let your gaze turn into an unsettling stare. Feel free to look away for a moment when you are changing a subject, offering a verbal nod, recalling information or when the other person does.

It's not just making eye contact that is important – your eyes are an important focus in many ways. If you wear glasses normally, wear them now and ensure they are clean; dirty lenses can make anyone look slovenly no matter how sharp their suit is. If you are a frequent blinker, try to regulate the habit or people may assume you are edgy and would rather not talk. Even if you are exhausted, try not to rub your eyes – doing so can make you look overwhelmed.

Are you sitting comfortably?

Although networking events largely rely on freedom of movement around a room, you may find yourself at business or social events where you will be in seated conversation for some of the time. Even in situations like these, it is possible to adapt your body language in a way that makes you feel confident and make you look more open to approach by others. That word *open* is key. Remove things from table tops that obstruct the view between you and other people. Resist the temptation to cross your arms – instead rest your hands on your thigh or loosely clasp them on the table top if there is one. Keep your hands away from your mouth and face. Crossing your legs is fine but (men) avoid the overconfident 'ankle on knee' look that spreads the legs, pushes the bottom forward and results in an over-relaxed sprawl.

Your body can send out a strong body language message: the smile might be perfectly relaxed, but the drumming fingers or tapping foot say otherwise. Remember that your whole body can reveal how you are feeling, and it's the parts you consider least important that offer others the clearest insight. If your legs are uncrossed, keep your feet flat on the floor – tipped or angled feet look tense and you may be tempted to jiggle them nervously.

Holding your head up and your shoulders back is even more important when sitting, as a slumped posture in a chair creates a very 'closed' appearance – people next to you will find it very difficult to strike up conversation. Instead look up, look animated, still your body movements and have the very beginnings of a smile on your face. You will fool yourself into self-confidence, and you won't be alone for long.

Key take-aways

Write down the things you will take from Step 4 and how you will implement them.

Topic	Take-away	Implementation
The four types of listener	• *Non-listener* • *Marginal listener* • *Pretend listener* • *Active listener*	• *Be more aware of pitfalls like planning what I want to say instead of listening.*
Improve your listening skills with active listening		
How to build good relationships in conversation and business writing		
How to use FACE to show empathy		
Understand the five key areas of personal experience		
Learn a 'small talk' format that works		
Improve your voice and vocabulary		
How to be confident in sustained conversation		
How to shake hands		
How to maintain appropriate eye contact		
How to stand with confidence		
How to sit with confidence		

Step 5

SURVIVE DIFFICULT MOMENTS

'Man is the only animal that blushes.
Or needs to.'
— Mark Twain (1835–1910), Author

Five ways to succeed

- Resolve mishaps quickly, quietly and decisively.
- If you arrive late, take some extra time.
- Get phone numbers if you forget business cards.
- Analyse your mistakes.
- Learn about the cultures of people you plan to meet.

Five ways to fail

- If you spill something, ignore it.
- Immediately drop unlikeable people from your network.
- Be rude if you meet rude people when networking.
- Never own up to forgetting someone's name.
- Don't learn languages to network internationally.

Deal with anything

Networking brings you together with people you perhaps wouldn't otherwise meet. Meeting people from other walks of life provides an opportunity for learning, and for forcing you to examine the appropriateness of your own opinions and behaviours.

Networking also involves presenting yourself as an ambassador for yourself or for your company, which means you are also trying to come across as someone who is professional, has integrity and who both gives and deserves respect.

So, you have to be at the top of your game in some challenging contexts. We'll look at some ways of picking your way through this minefield. However, no amount of specific advice can rival the importance of basic, human courtesy in all interactions. When other answers fail you, remember these key points:

■ **Do as you would be done by:** be courteous to your fellow man.

■ **Be sensitive:** pay attention to how others appear to be feeling.

■ **Be flexible:** being inflexible is what often causes most offence.

■ **Learn:** don't let your networking potential be compromised by ignorance of other cultures.

■ **Be responsive:** always be willing to defuse, apologize and remedy any situation you have caused.

Dealing with practical mishaps

We are all human, and humans make mistakes. But the important thing when networking is to present the best version of yourself at all times. So what do you do when something happens that makes you look like a bit of an idiot? The simple answer is damage limitation, and here's how:

Spilled food or drink on someone?

First, claim responsibility, apologize unreservedly, and be sincere about it. Then, prevent the mishap from becoming a spectacle by removing yourself and the other person from the interested gaze of others. Ask the person to come with you so you can help them clean up and offer to pay for any resulting laundry bill in private. If moving to another room (or the loos) isn't an option, at the very least take the person out of the immediate area. Even moving a few paces will prevent onlookers from watching the proceedings.

Spilled food or drink on yourself?

If you did this in public, don't try to ignore the fact you have mustard down your lapel and continue talking. No matter how good your pitch is, or how good a listener you are, it will be that stain everyone remembers, not you. Briefly acknowledge what's happened immediately, have a laugh about it so others can relax about the fact they've noticed, then remove the offending article from view – and from the discussion. If you've spilt something on a jacket or cardigan, remove it and put it away. If it's your tie, remove the tie and open your top button. Then get back to your topic of conversation without hesitation. If you've messed up a skirt or trousers, leave the conversation at an appropriate juncture and head to the loos to see if you can remedy things. Though you may feel like it, resist the urge to just make an embarrassed bolt for the door, abandoning all your efforts so far. Whenever you feel ready to resume conversation, make a concerted effort to introduce a new topic and make improved eye contact. Both of these tactics will aid your recovery. The person with whom you're speaking will be able to re-engage with you on a fresh footing, rather than staying distracted by the incident before. Whatever you do, don't go on about it; you are only drawing attention to your own clumsiness and embarrassment, neither of which are desirable business attributes and shouldn't be advertised.

Being late

If the traffic has conspired against you and you arrive late, the best tactic – surprisingly – may be to take yet a little more time out to calm down before you enter an event. Five minutes either way makes little difference to others, yet could provide a total facesaver for you. When we're late, our heart rate rises, we get sweaty, we start pulling things out of bags and briefcases to check maps and phones, and don't put them back properly. The result is, you arrive out of breath, perspiring, red faced and with your belongings all in a muddle – not a good look. Take five minutes in the toilets or cloakroom to get your things back in order, straighten up your clothes and hair, and wash your face and hands if necessary. Then you can enter, looking like nothing has happened. If you've a meeting arranged with someone for whom you're now late, you should let them know that you are here. If they're now in conversation with someone else, wait for an appropriate moment to introduce yourself (more on that in Step 6). Apologize for your lateness, briefly explain why it happened, and then ask the person whether they are still free to talk now, or would like to rearrange. What is key to a successful recovery is to briefly (but sincerely) apologize before getting *off* the subject of your lateness. You want your new contact to remember what you had to say, not the fact you were late.

Forgetting a vital piece of equipment

In the middle of showing someone your new product range on your laptop you run out of battery and have forgotten your leads – or some other vital piece of kit. But how to handle this when it happens? Well, the same tactic applies as for clothing mishaps and lateness. Apologize for your oversight, then put away the equipment – don't dither. Be clear and decisive. Explain you don't have what you need and turn the conversation away from that. Now's the perfect time to offer your business card and point potential customers to your website. It may even give you the springboard to suggest lunch during the week. Whatever you do, don't act the victim; take positive action to dispel the negative moment.

Forgetting business cards

Though they seem such a networking staple, it's not a disaster if you forget business cards. If asked for one, don't own up to having forgotten cards but instead say 'Sorry – I just handed out my last one.' Then use the opening to get your phones out, swap numbers and arrange a call or hook up on LinkedIn®. If you have a smartphone, explore the many apps out there that allow you to bump phones and swap contact details, or create your own virtual business cards. Many networking veterans would say that occasionally having no business cards can be a good exercise – forcing you to become a proactive networker who is able to think on their feet.

Prevention is better than cure

Though it's handy to know what to do in a crisis, prevention is undeniably better than cure. Make it a priority to prevent disasters rather than becoming adept at sorting them out. Here's how.

- **Acknowledge your weaknesses:** If you know you're forgetful, face it: make lists of what you need and schedule phone/email alerts to check them before events. If you tend to be clumsy, minimize calamity: don't wear a light-cream suit, then drink cranberry juice, eat red pesto and expect to get out unscathed. Invest in darker colours, drink water and choose 'neat' food that won't make marks. You wouldn't eat spag bol on a first date, would you?

- **Be decisive:** When unavoidable mistakes do happen, act decisively; don't prolong the agony, mutter incomprehensibly and make yourself a spectacle while you're at it. It's like driving – if you don't know what to do on a roundabout, don't change your mind mid-manoeuvre. Make a decision, and carry out that manoeuvre clearly and decisively. So too with networking; acknowledge the mistake, say how you're going to deal with it, do that, and move on.

- **Review your behaviour:** After the event, take time to work out why mistakes happened. Did you knock someone's drink over them? Why? Perhaps you wave your hands about too much when you are nervous about talking? Were you horribly late? Why? Perhaps you need to spend more time planning your travel. Learn from mistakes, don't repeat them.

Difficult conversations

How do we deal with situations that are forced on us by our interactions with other people? The more you network, the more you are going to run into people who are very different from you in outlook, ideas and opinions. That proves you are networking effectively. Some of these people will be easy to get along with. Others may not be so easy, but that doesn't necessarily mean that they should not be included in your network. Your challenge is to become someone who can find value in most people and can smooth over the bumps in most social situations.

How to handle difficult people in conversation

There will be times when, once you've introduced yourself to someone started conversation, you wish you hadn't. The person is rude and cynical. But what if you need them as a contact? You can't always ditch new contacts just because they're unlikeable. In such cases, you may have to learn some techniques that can make interaction more fruitful, now and for the future.

■ **Don't counter-attack; ask questions:** Extending what we've learned about active listening in Step 4, this can be particularly helpful when dealing with someone who is opinionated or argumentative. If, say, you've just mentioned that you work in recycling and your new contact says 'recycling is a waste of time and money,' resist a squabble, but instead, gently ask them to elaborate: 'In what ways is it a waste?' This way, they're likely to identify the flaws in their own argument without conflict between you.

■ **Stay calm and polite:** If someone is being rude to you, don't mirror their behaviour, or what began as a difficult conversation could escalate to a big argument. By staying calm you will defuse any potential aggression and also (eventually) gain the respect of the other.

■ **Side-step unacceptable behaviour:** If someone is racist or sexist, it's unlikely you will ever want to work with them. Don't counter, or even acknowledge, their outdated views, but respond with silence. At an appropriate juncture, excuse yourself and move on. See Step 6 for polite ways to do this.

■ **Don't take nastiness personally:** Some people are impossible to please, and can come across as brusque, cynical and rude. If you meet someone like this while networking it's highly unlikely that their sharp demeanour has anything to do with you. Accepting that some people just have unpleasant personalities makes it easier not to take it personally. Taking things personally will only make it harder for you every time you have to deal with them. Work on growing a thick skin for yourself.

■ **Avoid the 'you' word:** the pronoun 'you' is very personal and can sound like an attack. If, for example, you mention you are a social media consultant, and they say 'I'll never use social media because it's just a passing craze', you could enrage someone by saying 'You're wrong' or 'Your opinion is wrong'. Instead, use a more neutral sentence like 'there is evidence against that argument' or turn it to yourself using 'I', such as 'I think that social media is here to stay'. Then you are countering the actual issue, not the *person*.

■ **Create a bell-jar for yourself:** When all else fails, a little visualisation won't go amiss when dealing with a particularly abrasive person. Imagine yourself in conversation with this person as you are now, but a large bell-jar placed over your head protects you from their nasty comments. Listen to their disagreeable remarks pinging off the glass without any effect on you. Try it; it works!

What to do when people don't want to talk to you

There will come a time when you are at a networking event and you find yourself struggling to make conversation with someone who clearly doesn't want to talk. Perhaps the most important thing to do in a situation like this is to take your time, don't jump to conclusions and don't abandon ship too quickly – the person may be painfully shy or have just received some bad news. Persevere with one or two open questions such as 'How are you enjoying the event?' or 'Where have you come from today?' to gently encourage the person into a fuller response. If, after a few such questions from you, you are still getting one-word, dead-end answers, then it may be time to politely move on. Using a phrase like 'I'm sure you have lots of people you'd like to meet, so I'd best let you go' is a positive way of giving the reluctant person an escape route. Whatever you do, don't be rude. Networking is all about building bridges, not burning them. So be polite, extricate yourself with dignity and forget about what just happened. It is very important that you don't take such rebuffs personally – you have no way of knowing what that other person is feeling. It is unlikely that it has anything to do with you, so just take a deep breath, have a glass of water, and go meet someone more talkative.

What do to when you forget someone's name

We've all done it. And it's even more forgivable if you're at a social or networking event where you've been inundated with new names for the past hour or so. But do sort out your mental blank as soon as possible. Avoiding using each other's names is not an option – the blank spaces in conversation soon become achingly obvious and prevent dialogue from going anywhere meaningful. The best idea is to act immediately:

- If it's an informal event, you can discreetly ask the host for any names that you have forgotten.

- Be totally up front and say, 'I'm so sorry but I have forgotten your name' or, 'I'm sorry, but I don't think I got your name when we were introduced'.

- If you know you've met before, take the bull by the horns and reintroduce yourself first, saying something like 'I'm Mark – we met a while back and I wasn't sure if you'd remember me'. Nine times out of ten the other person will reciprocate with their own name. Then you can breathe a huge sigh of relief!

- If the person has an unusual name that is difficult to pronounce, do ask them how to spell it or to check your pronunciation. This is much more courteous than hearing their name once and getting it wrong thereafter.

A person's name is the essence of their identity. Asking someone to repeat their name is positive – it shows you value both the person and their name.

Ice-breakers and ice-makers

When we are in conversation, even in a business environment, it is natural to meander through topics as dialogue unfolds. To support and prolong conversation, we often fill gaps between the more serious stuff with small talk, conversation that touches on topics we enjoy or find easy to talk about. These topics often include sport, the weather and our families. They normally provide a fail-safe way of breaking the ice in a relationship. However, when you are networking abroad or with people of many different nationalities, it is vital to be sensitive to topics that different cultures prefer to avoid. What may be your idea of an ice-breaker may just be someone else's 'ice-maker', and could stop a conversation and a business relationship in its tracks.

If you are in an environment where there are people of many different nationalities, take care with the following topics in conversation:

- Partners and families

- Differences in the status of men and women

- National politics, national success or national heroes

- Relationships with neighbouring countries

- Language diversity within a country

- Religion and religious differences

- Sport and associated rivalries

- Wealth and social status or property and possession

Sounding Pro: How to deal with sensitive topics

All of the topics on page 97 are 'cultural faultlines' – subjects that can divide opinion between people of different societies. Yet, networking in multi-cultural environments may mean you need to discuss these subjects to do business effectively. Be reassured; you can approach most things without causing offence if you acquire tactful vocabulary to help you tread carefully.

How to ask about sensitive subjects	*Would you mind if I asked you about the political situation?*
	Could I ask you a delicate question?
How to avoid difficult or sensitive subjects	*Would it be okay if we talk about something else?*
	Do you mind at all if we don't talk about that?
How to agree to talking about a sensitive subject	*Not at all. Go ahead.*
	Ask away./Feel free.
	No problem. What would you like to know?
How to apologize if you raise a sensitive area in conversation	*I'm so sorry if I've said the wrong thing.*
	I think I've offended you. If I have I'm really sorry.

If you cause offence, apologize immediately and move off the topic. Moving physically can also have a clearing effect – suggest getting a glass of water, or ask the person to come to meet one of your colleagues.

Cultural etiquette: dos and taboos

While diversity brings opportunity, it also brings challenges, as we have seen. Understanding and respecting cultural differences can have a positive effect on your business interactions. But it goes beyond sensitive topics of conversation.

Etiquette is an unwritten set of rules that governs how we conduct ourselves. When we get it right, etiquette smoothes interaction, even in unfamiliar circumstances. When we get it wrong, offence is taken and people can get upset. Cast your mind back to the last time someone jumped a queue in front of you, or let the door go behind them instead of holding it for you. These are simple breaches of etiquette that make us tetchy. But it's vital to remember that some breaches of international etiquette cut to the very heart of gender difference and religious belief: the offended parties are going to be a little more than grumpy!

The following information may give you a starting point for further research. It may also make you act with a little more tact in all transactions, which must surely be a good thing. Let's look at how to equip yourself for international networking, and the areas you should approach with care.

Cultural complacency is no joke

Making one simple mistake in international etiquette could cause serious offence. If you are planning international networking, ensure you do three key things.

■ **Research:** Learn as much as you can about the culture of the people you are going to visit or work with. Travel guides, the Internet and the country's embassy will all have information on etiquette.

■ **Learn vital words:** Learn how to say 'hello', 'goodbye', 'please', 'thank you' and 'sorry'. Practise any physical greetings you will need e.g., how to bow in Japan, or make the *namaskar* (the palms are brought together and thumbs raised to the forehead as the head and upper body are inclined in a bow) in India.

■ **Go with the flow:** The saying 'When in Rome, do as the Romans do' is great advice for international networking. Try to ease into the culture and respectfully try new things.

Business card etiquette: In the UK we often exchange business cards while continuing to talk, burying them into wallets or back pockets while conversation continues. If you did this to someone from China or Japan however, it would come across as a personal affront. Instead, every effort should be made to give and receive business cards with both hands. The card should then be read with interest, must not be put away until the end of the conversation, and never in a pocket. In Asian, African, and Middle Eastern countries, it is offensive to receive a card with your left hand. In many countries, the business card generally demands more respect than it does here, so if you are networking with people from different cultures, invest in an attractive business card holder, treat cards with respect, and never write on one in public.

Personal space: Boundaries of acceptable personal space vary minutely from person to person, and can vary hugely from one culture to another. In many cultures, the boundaries of personal space are very complex, so if you are taken aback either by a person's physical forwardness or aloofness, always take a moment to consider that this may be a cultural norm, rather than a personality trait of one individual. In many countries, it is normal for men to be close and very tactile, but to make contact with women in a similar way would be considered taboo. It's complex; you should research this carefully if networking internationally.

Gender differences: The place of women varies from one culture to another, so it's imperative to do your homework. In Denmark, women are greeted before men, while in Russia, women may be overlooked entirely. In the Middle East, men may place their hand on their chest rather than accept the handshake of a woman. Find out what happens where you're going.

Dress: In many cultures women must not bare their arms or shoulders, and to do so in public would constitute a religious and moral affront. Women networking internationally should consider wearing long-sleeved dresses or skirt suits, opting for solid, muted colours and avoiding boots, very high heels or open-toed shoes. Think twice about wearing expensive jewellery in high-risk areas too.

Hierarchy: Some nations, in particular Japan and China, place great emphasis on hierarchy, so seating arrangements will usually be made according to 'rank'. Be aware of this when attending meetings (or even climbing into cabs) in international contexts – wait until others are seated or you are allocated a place.

Punctuality: While occasional lateness is tolerated in many European cultures, being tardy in, say, India or Japan would be considered highly irregular, and may even cause concern. Always allow extra time when meeting international contacts – lateness may cause grave offence.

Gift-giving: Gift giving in an international context should be undertaken with care. In Saudi Arabia, exchanging gifts is strictly reserved for close friends, while in China and Japan, business gifts are appreciated, yet will be modestly refused initially, and must be reciprocated.

Sounding Pro: Letters of apology

No matter how good your intentions, there may be times when you mess up an element of international etiquette. It's vital to apologize unreservedly on the spot, but also worthwhile sending a follow-up letter of apology too. That may be nerve-wracking, so here are four simple steps to guide you.

Paragraph 1: **Pleasure**	Express what a pleasure it was to meet the other person.
Paragraph 2: **Problem**	Describe what you think the problem is.
Paragraph 3: **Explanation and apology**	Explain the reasons for what you did and apologize for any rudeness.
Paragraph 4: **Intention**	Say what you mean to do in the future.

So using the steps above, an appropriate letter of apology may look something like this:

Dear ...

It was a great pleasure to see you again and thank you so much for inviting me to dinner at your lovely home.

I am concerned that during the meal I may have caused offence by asking questions about your wife and family. Please excuse me if I did.

It is normal to ask about partners and families in my country and, unthinkingly, I did the same in your house. I'm extremely sorry if I said the wrong thing. I did not mean to cause offence and hope you will understand the reasons for my mistake.

Thank you again for the wonderful evening and delicious food; I look forward to returning your hospitality and seeing you very soon.

Best regards,
Simon

Key take-aways

Think about the things you will take away from Step 5 and how
you will implement them.

Topic	Take-away	Implementation
Become more able to deal with any kind of social mishap or challenge	• *Use common sense.* • *Exercise courtesy.*	• *Treat others the way I would like to be treated.* • *Be more sensitive.* • *Be more responsive.*
Dealing with practical mishaps		
How to prevent rather than resolve mishaps		
Coping with difficult people		
How to cope when people don't want to talk		
What to do when you forget someone's name		
Identifying ice-breakers and ice-makers		
How to avoid causing offence		
Cultural differences in etiquette		
Avoiding cultural complacency		
How to write a letter of apology		

Step 6

WORK THE ROOM

'I've always been in the right place and time.
Of course, I steered myself there.'
— Bob Hope (1903–2003), Actor

Five ways to succeed

- Prepare to network – use your voice en route.
- Walk once around the room to prepare.
- Assume that everyone has little time.
- Be upfront about beneficial mutual introductions.
- Help people on their own to integrate.

Five ways to fail

- Force your way into closed groups.
- Be blunt with hangers-on.
- Sit with the people you know best.
- Approach a must-have contact without hesitation.
- Take time to give details of your business.

Getting into conversation

Warming up

To work at your best you need to warm up your voice, attitude and smile before you go in – just a few minutes' preparation can make all the difference. So, pop a mint in your mouth and off we go.

- **Get talkative:** Talk in the car, tell jokes to yourself, sing. In a taxi? Have a chat with your cabby. If you came on public transport, arrive early at the venue and talk to the cloakroom attendant. Get into the swing of talking freely.

- **Have a couple of the day's headlines to hand:** Remember one serious and one celeb/gossip news item to whip out when you need to fill a gap or revive a reluctant conversation. You can be the judge of which to use when needed.

- **Arrive early:** As well as getting you started before any cliques start to appear, some networking observers also believe that arriving early instils a host mentality: you acclimatize to the venue layout before anyone else, and adopt the confident behaviour of a meeter and greeter.

- **Put your name tag on your right lapel:** that puts it in the line of sight when you are shaking someone's hand.

Plan your journey through the room

Many networkers advocate walking around the room once before you do anything. A walk around helps you make better choices and plan your time effectively. So what are you looking for in your walk-through?

- **Locate the people you plan to meet:** Are they here yet? Prioritize the people you must meet and make a mental list of those you'd like to. When the time comes you can approach with purpose, rather than stumbling upon them unprepared and peering at their name tags.

- **Find any guest speakers you hope to meet:** Introduce yourself early before they make their presentation – afterwards they'll be lost in a sea of people asking questions.

- **Identify groups of three or more, and people standing alone:** These will be the most receptive to you joining them.

- **Find the busiest spot:** When you are in between planned meetings, or need help to get started, hang out there, where you are most likely to make or receive an impromptu introduction.

- **Locate any food:** Something about the shared activity of choosing food makes us drop our guard, becoming receptive to small talk and comment – enough to jumpstart a conversation.

Once you've done these things, you can form a blueprint in your mind of how your morning might shape up. Yes, serendipitous meetings may cut across that, but if none appear, you now have a loose plan of how you are going to tackle the room, and what to do if introductions are slow. Keep moving!

How to move into conversations that seem closed

When approaching a group look out for some 'welcoming' signs. A group that is open to new additions may have physical space in it for others. Its members might even stand loosely apart, and at an angle to each other. Are their faces still visible to passers-by? Perhaps one or two of the group are pointing a foot out of the circle, as if to break it. If you see a few of these signs, you may well be greeted warmly. Approach quietly, smile, and look interested. Wait for a break in conversation or until someone catches your eye to invite you in. If either happens, you've been accepted. Say something like 'May I join you?' and you're sorted. If people's backs form a barrier, their feet point to each other, they maintain eye contact and ignore your presence, don't attempt to break the seal. Move on and try again later.

Getting out of conversation

As important as it is to get into conversation, it's often equally important to get out of the ones that are going nowhere. But how do you do that?

Knowing when someone is finished speaking to you

In most cases you will realise when someone is ready to move on from conversation with you. In case you don't see the signs, here's a reminder:

- **Restlessness:** When someone who has been previously attentive starts to shuffle around a little, straighten their tie, or shift their weight from one foot to another.

- **Angling outward:** When people begin to point their body and/or feet away from the conversation with you, they're ready to leave or welcome a new addition into it.

- **Loss of eye contact:** The other person may start to erode eye contact, glance furtively over your shoulder, or at a watch or phone.

- **Closed questions and answers:** When someone begins to use closed questions that demand only a 'yes/no' from you, or begin to respond in this way.

- **Closing phrases:** Redundant phrases that say nothing new are a dead giveaway. Statements like 'Well, that's really helpful', or an overt use of the past tense such as 'This has been so interesting' indicate that the conversation is over.

How to finish conversations politely

So, a number of the telltale signs are becoming obvious. The thing to do when someone is itching to get away is to let them go with generosity. (You're building bridges, not burning them, remember.) It's gracious to do two things:

■ claim sole responsibility for holding the other person up;

■ imply that the other person's time is more precious than yours.

So, you may end up saying something along the lines of: 'Goodness, I've kept you back far too long, you must have so many people still to meet'. This way, you are gifting an exit strategy while gently underlining their perceived importance. You let them go, and massage their ego a bit on the way.

When the shoe is on the other foot and you are the one trying to extricate yourself, conclude the conversation with friendliness and all will be well.

■ Close decisively, but reassure them that you've taken something good from the conversation, e.g. 'I've really enjoyed speaking with you – I've learned a lot about ...'

■ Apologize, say you have to go and explain why. A proper explanation is essential if you want to be courteous. Compare 'I'm sorry, but I must go; there is someone here from logistics that I'm keen to meet before he leaves,' with 'Excuse me, I must go'. Which would you rather have?

Extricating yourself

Hangers-on waste your time and they compromise your freedom to meet other people. Allowing them to follow you around isn't helping them either – it's likely that once they've learned this habit they'll use it every time they 'network'. So, be cruel to be kind and get them moving.

■ **Remind them everyone is here to network:** At a break in the conversation, suggest that the two of you move off together to meet some new faces. To be polite, suggest you've been at fault, saying something like 'Goodness, I've kept you back for thirty minutes – shall we mingle?'

■ **Point out people they might want to meet:** Because it's likely you've spent some time together, you'll know what their interests are. Point out people that may be useful for them to meet.

■ **Wait for them to integrate:** Never leave someone on their own. If they don't take the hints above, take them with you to join another group. Introduce yourself to the group, then allow your companion to introduce themselves too. When they settle in, it's okay for you to move on. Apologize briefly, say that it's been nice to meet them, and explain why you must go. Job done.

Sounding Pro: Navigating through conversations

Over time, you will develop your own favoured toolkit of polite phrases to get in and out of conversation. Until then, here are a few suggestions. Observe how other networkers handle awkward situations, so you can learn from their mistakes and successes too.

Moving into conversations that seem closed	*I'm sorry to interrupt but I'm very interested in what you're discussing.*
	Excuse me, could I possibly join you at all?
Releasing someone who looks like they would like to, or need to, get away	*I'm sure you have to get on, I'm sorry if I've held you up.*
Closing a conversation politely when you need to leave	**Reiterating the benefits you are taking from the conversation:**
	I'm glad we met today. This has been very useful.
	Apologizing, explaining you have to go and why:
	I'm afraid you'll have to excuse me – I have to do a bit of prep for a meeting later. I hope the rest of your morning goes well.
Extricating yourself from hangers-on	*I've held you back much too long – perhaps we could go together and meet some new faces?'*
	Didn't you say you were interested in [field]? I could introduce you to [name] right over there. I'm sure he could be really helpful.

Working with the unexpected

Networking will rarely go according to any fixed plan. The trick is learning to cope with and get the best out of just about anything, and to seize opportunities when they appear.

Don't rush off

While we've learned that it's rude to leave someone standing on their own, there may nevertheless come a time when *you're* abandoned suddenly with no clue what to do next. Possibly the best advice is not to scurry off heedlessly. Take a breath, smile, and review the room as you did on arrival: look for others on their own; locate the food (if there is food), where people are invariably relaxed; or identify the busiest area. Then, head for one of these places and flip that negative moment into positive action.

Don't rush in

You spot someone across the room that you've wanted to meet for years. You rush straight over, but when you get there, words fail you with embarrassing results – nightmare. Next time, take a deep breath and pause for a moment before you do anything. Rehearse in your mind how you are going to introduce yourself and what you would like to say. Then make your approach with confidence.

Haven't we met before?

If you spot someone whose face you recognize, but can't place where from, use it to your advantage. Feel free to approach them and be honest about it. You can say something like 'I hope you don't mind me introducing myself, but I'm pretty sure we've met before – may I ask your name again?' People are – for the most part – helpful and will meet you halfway in such conversations, introducing themselves and offering snippets of background information to jog your memory. At the end of the day it doesn't even matter if you find out that you were wrong and you haven't met. By the time you establish this, the conversation will be in full swing, you will have exchanged valuable information about each other, maybe even had a bit of a giggle at your mistake too – and there's nothing more bonding than laughter.

We have to stop meeting like this

We've all experienced it; you are in a social situation and keep bumping into the same person again, to the point where you start to have a joke about it. Well, some networking veterans actually advocate this, saying that coming back to someone briefly for a second time (no more) in one event can instil a feeling of camaraderie – like you've known each other for a while. It's not a technique to roadtest at your first event, but once you're getting used to networking it may well come in handy to cement a fledgling relationship with a valuable contact.

Mobility at seated events

What about those situations where you are seated, say at a dinner or listening to a guest speaker? Well, the aim is the same – maximising your exposure to new people. Here's how.

Choose a seat nowhere near anyone you know

Resist the temptation to sit with a friend or colleague across the room. You would have a nice time, but you will invariably become lost in conversation and speak to no one new. Similarly, you and your colleague(s) will appear closed to others with the result that even those sitting next to you will find it hard to break into the conversation.

Resist the temptation to stick with a new contact

It may seem natural to prolong a chat with someone new by taking it to the dinner or conference seating and sitting down together. Make sure you know what you are getting into. Sitting together guarantees a long stretch in each other's company, and your new contact (or you) may feel suffocated by that prospect. If you prefer, you can break conversation before people start heading towards seating. 'Let's catch up again after dinner/the presentation' is decisive but positive, so no offence should be taken.

Introduce yourself to everyone around

If you are seated at a table for a dinner event, introduce yourself to everyone who sits down. Break the ice by passing the menu round for them to see, pouring water, discussing the venue, or even what your food choices are going to be. Taking part in the housekeeping duties of the table also imparts that 'host physiology' we came across earlier, which in itself will give you confidence, allow you to move a bit more, and free up your body language, rather than sitting in silence with your hands clasped anxiously in your lap. Be tactful however, if you are at an event where individual tables are hosted by sponsoring companies. In such cases, be careful not to tread on the toes of the delegate who is hosting your table, they will probably have paid quite a bit of cash for the honour.

Make the most of intervals

If there are intervals between speakers, or long breaks between courses, use them. Don't be tempted to sit tight to read notes or check your phone. The beauty of such intervals is that they are finite, you have an exit strategy (i.e. the seat you have to return to), and you have bags to talk about, whether it be the speaker, food, or the venue. Get up, move around and use the few precious minutes you have to meet someone new. Intervals are 'networking made easy', so use every second to maximize your mobile time.

Sit opposite rather than beside

Many of us instinctively sit beside the people we want to speak to, regardless of the fact that holding a conversation side by side is horribly awkward. If you really want to engage someone in conversation, sit opposite them (unless of course, it's a very wide table). That way, you can make proper eye contact, sit more naturally, and the messy details of eating while talking will not be quite so 'up close and personal' as they would be next to you. Quietly move aside any menus or table arrangements that obscure your view of each other. You will be able to read and project facial expressions much more accurately from here, instead of getting a compromised and uninformative side view. Sitting face-on has more positive impact, looks more professional, and will save you a bit of neck strain too.

Keep your hands free

Staying mobile and open to shaking hands can become problematic if you don't know what to do with the things you have to carry, so be careful when networking that you don't create unintentional barriers between yourself and introductions.

Food and glasses

When you are moving through a non-seated networking event, it's a good idea not to carry a glass and a plate of food at the same time, as you won't be free to shake hands or receive a business card (especially if you are in China or Japan). Plan for this. By all means have a drink with you, but try to carry it in your left hand so that you can shake hands. If you want to eat, plan to do it as an isolated item on your networking agenda, rather than dragging food round the event with you.

Business cards

Do you have somewhere to put other people's cards without mixing them up with your own? Invest in a business suit or bag that has pockets for outgoing and incoming business cards, one pocket for each type.

Keeping the room mobile

We've established that contemporary networking thrives not on the selfish pursuit of what you want, but the 'pay it forward' mentality: giving first without expectation. This attitude of helping others applies to all aspects of networking, not least in taking group responsibility for keeping the whole room moving and meeting.

Set timescales

Assume that you only have ten minutes tops with anyone, and that you need to say the crucial stuff within that timescale. If you both want to linger, that's great. Just don't take it for granted.

Tailor detail to the time available

A good elevator pitch gives the person you're with a concise overview of what you do, while whetting their appetite to find out more. In response to a compelling pitch they're likely to ask open-ended questions such as 'How does that work?' etc. In your reply, remember that you're not closing a deal here, but offering enticing high-level details only; time is precious. Offer to explain things in more detail after the event, and use that opportunity to offer your business card and arrange a meeting to continue the conversation.

Engage with everyone in group conversation

To keep conversation fluid, it's important that group conversations find some level of balance. If you are in a group conversation, try to engage with every member of that group, however briefly. This levels the playing field amongst all members, and opens the floor to all, making for richer conversations and more fruitful connections. When one individual assumes a dominant role in a group it can make conversation one-sided, encourage submissive 'interview-style' responses from others, and make movement away from the group more difficult to achieve. Proceed with tact, however, if a VIP assumes this role in a group – competing with them may not be the best tactic for your career advancement. Instead, allow them to hold court, asking open questions and engaging other members of the group when you can.

Look out for and welcome loners

If you spot someone alone, help them out by introducing yourself. There may be little or no business value in it whatsoever, but it will bolster both your self-confidence and theirs. Once you have got them talking, introduce them onward to another group or person you met previously (using the techniques we learned on page 91), giving them a springboard into another conversation and yourself a polite and appropriate exit point. Once they're settled, you can leave. You look professional and magnanimous to both them and the wider group, they get an easy couple of introductions. Everybody wins, and you will feel pretty darned good about yourself too.

Facilitate mutual introductions

Mutual introduction is when you introduce someone you know to an established contact. When you make a mutual introduction, you are quietly endorsing the new person you are presenting. Others are likely to trust them more quickly, and will feel some (gentle) social pressure to accept them.

Ask for introductions

If there is someone you would like to meet at an event, and you have a mutual acquaintance, be upfront and ask them to introduce you. Upon introduction, the three of you will spend time working out how you've come to know each other. The next time you meet your new contact alone, you will have all that heritage behind you, giving you the beginnings of a trusting relationship.

Facilitate introductions

If a contact tells you that they'd love to meet someone in the room that you know, offer to introduce them. When you do, offer a short, positive description of how their interests relate to your other contact, e.g. 'Martin, I'd like you to meet Lynne; she's in HR and interested in your research on employment law.' This gives both people a springboard into conversation while gently underlining the fact that you are generous and professional.

Connect people outside of the event

The offer to make mutual introductions does not apply solely to the networking event; you should also be willing to bring people together in the days or weeks to follow. If someone you meet at an event would like to meet an established contact of yours who is absent, offer to phone or email that contact as a preliminary introduction. We will find out the protocols of this in *Step 7*. Offering to, and carrying out, such a favour not only makes you look well-connected and generous, but cements the relationship with the person you've just met at the event. Don't, however, offer to make such a gesture if you don't intend to follow through – your new contact won't trust you again.

Exercise caution

Mutual introductions are calculated risks. Introducing two people you know and trust presents little or no risk, and can enrich your network by opening up pathways to new people and cementing the relationships already present. However, if you meet someone at an event and intend to introduce them on, you have a duty of care to ensure you are not passing on a problem. Get a feel for their professionalism and trustworthiness before you promise anything. Trust your instincts, and avoid making promises to someone you are at all unsure of. Although it is always good to widen your network, you must look after your existing contacts first. Don't encumber your strong ties with people that you wish you'd never met.

The end is just the start

Try to remember two things at the end of a networking event:

- **You're not here to close deals:** You only need to leave an event with a mental list of those people who share common interests and goals with you. This will provide the foundation of mutually beneficial relationships later.

- **Not every new contact becomes valuable:** You may meet some interesting new people and arrange to follow up with all of them, or just a few. Follow-up is a 'selection' phase: not all of these contacts will become active members of your network. Gaining just one great contact from an event is a success story.

Key take-aways

Think about the things you will take away from Step 6 and how you will implement them.

Topic	Take-away	Implementation
Preparing yourself for networking conversation	• *Chat before the event* • *Check the news* • *Arrive early*	• *Plan a breakfast meeting before my next networking event* • *Check news headlines online in the morning*
The journey through a networking event		
Moving into closed conversations		
Knowing when to finish a conversation		
Concluding conversations politely		
Freeing yourself from hangers-on		
Coping with the unexpected		
Staying mobile at seated events		
Keeping your hands free		
Keeping the whole room mobile		
Facilitating mutual introductions		
The end of an event is the first step in building relationships		

Step 7

FOLLOW UP ON LEADS

*A man, sir, should keep
his friendship in constant repair.'
— Samuel Johnson (1709–84), Author*

Five ways to succeed

- Finish talking when you both have more to say.
- Thank people for speaking to you.
- Plan regular contact with members of your network.
- Learn how to ask for and accept help.
- Let go of stagnant relationships.

Five ways to fail

- Give your business card to everyone you meet.
- Send out group emails thanking everyone you meet.
- Never explain why you would like to meet someone.
- Only look after yourself.
- Continue relationships which have no mutual value.

Moving to the next phase

In the final step of this book we'll look at how crucial it is to nurture your network after each event – just as vital as being an exemplary event delegate, and probably more so in the long term.

What comes next is almost a filtration process: following up with the people you have met until you identify who is going to be with you for the long run, and who may bring lesser or no *mutual* benefit. Note the word mutual – you cannot add people to your network solely for their ability to provide you with value; relationships are two-way and both of you must benefit. In simple terms, the phrase 'I'll scratch your back and you scratch mine' still applies!

Buoyed by recent networking activity, it's easy to forget about your existing strong and weak ties – your diehards – who've been with you since before you even pinned a name badge on. That kind of oversight is forgivable briefly, but in the following pages we'll look at how to constantly review and tend your network so that nobody languishes unnoticed.

Let them know you want to talk more

Positive follow up begins before you have even picked up your coat to leave the event. It begins while you're still in conversation with your new contact, and (interestingly) while you feel you still have a lot more to say.

Mindful of people's schedules, it's courteous, as we've seen, to keep your conversations under ten minutes. In itself, this provides you with your opportunity for arranging further follow-up. You may, for example, say something like 'Actually, there's someone else I also have to speak to, and I'm sure you need to get away too – but I'd really like to talk more. Could I call or email you this week?' By keeping conversation to time you're effectively giving both of you a positive reason for further contact. Now is the time to swap business cards and close your conversation with the confidence that you have a new contact to follow up.

Swap business cards

To a great extent, successful networking relies on observing simple etiquette and acting courteously. The same goes for business card swapping. Forcing your card on people or being unthinking in other ways can potentially undermine all the hard work you've put in on your appearance, body language, and elevator pitch, no matter how well you've done so far. So, consider a few tactics that might help prevent disaster at the very last hurdle:

■ **Don't hand out your card lightly:** Pressing business cards on everyone you meet is a dead giveaway that you don't understand networking. Your business card is not a gift or a lottery ticket. Worthless on its own, the card itself is only as valuable as the exchange which precedes it. You should only hand out your card if there are clear benefits for both of you in doing so. Be selective.

■ **Ask outright if others can be contacted:** Good conversations inevitably reach a point where you want to talk more but time is pressing. At such points, asking the question 'Could I contact you during the week so we can talk more?' can propel the other person to hand over their card, ask for yours, and give you an action point to initiate follow up. Contrastingly, if you reach that same point in the conversation but say 'I'd really like to talk more, here's my card' without arranging contact, you have absolutely no guarantee that anything will come of the exchange.

■ **Always offer your card if asked for it:** It's always better to be asked than to be hasty in offering cards. Being asked for a card is a clear pointer that the person you are with places value on the interaction. So be prompt when asked, and make sure you know where it is – don't fumble through pockets to retrieve it, or you'll appear as if you've never done this in your life.

■ **Be careful about writing on business cards:** Many cultures treat business cards with great respect, and writing on someone else's card can be offensive. However, if you're at a large event and concluding a rewarding conversation, you may want to consider writing a short note on the back of your own business card before you hand it over. This could act as an aide-memoire for the other person – perhaps it's what you discussed: the title of a book or article that you recommended; or something that you promised to research for them. Never, ever, write anything that could be perceived as a demand. Only write a note if it's helpful and will jog the person's memory. Be very careful about making such notes when in a multi-cultural environment. Be sensitive to who you're with. If you have any concerns at all about whether they would find making a note on your card unusual or unsettling, just don't risk it.

■ **Make sure your card is up to date:** Crossed-out phone numbers are unacceptable.

End clearly and warmly

You've had a great conversation, swapped business cards and promised to catch up with each other. You're not out of the woods yet – let's ensure that you leave your new contact with a great impression.

- **Thank each other:** Never leave a rewarding conversation without thanking the other person for their time and insights. If you had a particularly rewarding conversation, don't let it end without offering some form of pre-emptive help to your new contact. This has to be relevant and appropriate: perhaps you could promise to forward an article on a related topic, or jot down the web address of an insightful blog. This smoothes the path to follow up, and demonstrates your professional generosity.

- **Give timescales:** If you've committed to contacting someone after the event, re-emphasize that you will be in touch and when you will be. This allows you to pick a time that works for you, while managing their expectations of timescales. Your new contact has an opportunity to say if that's a good time for them or not – always assume that their schedule is more crammed than yours.

- **Close with a handshake:** A good conversation should open with a firm hand-shake as we have seen in Step 3, but don't forget to close with one too. A closing handshake cements your new relationship with a mutual signal of agreement and trust – underlining that the conversation was satisfying for both of you. Even more simply, it's a clear 'finisher', making moving off much easier.

Thank the people you met

Back at your desk after networking, is the time to channel some of that new energy and optimism into shaping and nurturing your growing network, and it all starts with renewing contact.

Make your first follow up personal

■ **Say thank you:** Begin by emailing or calling those people that you talked to and received business cards from, to thank them for their time and prepare the way for further contact. Ideally, don't let more than 48 hours pass before doing this, (though you may have given some individuals more formal timescales for proper follow-up later). People will still remember you clearly at this stage, and early contact will keep you in the front of their minds longer.

■ **Build on a discussion point or offer some value:** You may, in the same conversation or email, want to expand on a discussion point you touched on in conversation, or offer value in other ways – in an email you could attach an article or a list of suppliers you promised. Whatever the medium, you may make an offer of direct help.

■ **Always send emails individually:** Never, ever, send out a group email to thank everyone you met. Every name on your list should be made to feel uniquely valuable.

■ **Err on the side of courtesy:** If you think that some of the connections you made don't have a future, it's still important and courteous to say thank you – you should strive to be remembered positively whatever the outcome.

Handwritten notes and when to use them

When reading about networking, you'll often be told that the best way to thank any contact after events is to send a handwritten note. While the final decision is yours, it's worthwhile to remember that business and social interaction is becoming increasingly immediate. While others may already have phoned, emailed, hooked up on LinkedIn® and entered the next phase of follow up, a handwritten note may still await delivery. However, most people will take the email route or similar, you can make yourself memorable by choosing to write such a note. This tactic can be effective to get the attention of a particularly valuable contact, or a VIP who is likely to have a swamped inbox or one filtered by a Personal Assistant. Letters are particularly appropriate after an exceptional event. Judge cases individually. Always be sincere and succinct. And be prompt – post first class.

Record information while it's fresh

After an event, you will have lots of information. This is useful stuff, so record it now, before you forget everything you've experienced.

Make notes about who you met

File your business cards properly. While doing so, make notes about each person who gave one to you. Note their specialist expertise. What are your initial thoughts about your value to them, and them to you? Could you introduce them to one of your existing contacts? All of this information can be recorded in a spreadsheet. Note the names of people you met, where you met them, their contact details and notes on how you will follow up with them.

Note your ideas

Did meeting new people fire your imagination and help you think creatively about your business field? Record these ideas! Explore them in a mind map, scrawl them on a white board or stick notes on your laptop.

Review what worked and what didn't

Did your elevator pitch sound compelling or did it fall flat? Did you flail a bit at making introductions? Identify those areas that you think worked well and any that need a rethink or some extra effort.

Create a follow-up plan

How do you ensure that you've got time to follow up with the people you've recently met? How do you continue to nourish relationships with people you've known a long time? Here's how:

The follow-up plan

■ **Plan for regular follow-up:** With your list of contacts, and your monthly (or quarterly) schedule to hand, make time (and budget) for key contacts, or other things will take over. Set yourself prompts for phoning, emailing and meeting up with people. Prioritize some people over others, but don't let any fall off your list unless you intend them to.

■ **Vary follow-up timing and type:** Avoid contacting people at the same point in the calendar all the time. Vary the ways in which you make contact too, ensuring they always offer value. You might phone with some useful business intelligence one week, email an interesting article the following month or endorse your contact on LinkedIn® at any moment.

■ **Contact will eventually become spontaneous:** Meticulously planning follow-up needn't last forever, but is crucial for getting new ties off the ground. When good new relationships deepen beyond deliberate acts of mutual exchange, they'll become more spontaneous, needing less planning to maintain.

Staying in touch with self-confidence

Keeping in regular dialogue with new contacts sounds straight-forward, but what if you find the whole process nerve-wracking? Be assured that many people will find follow up daunting, perhaps even more so than the event itself. Here are a few considerations that might help take away the fear.

- **You're not dating:** You're not dating your new contact, but building a mutually valuable business relationship, so rejection shouldn't be quite as terrifying a prospect. If you don't initially get a warm response from a follow-up message, don't take it personally. Try another way of getting in touch. And vary your message too.

- **Have an excuse:** Always give yourself a reason for getting in touch, and ensure it's valuable to your new contact. Opening with 'Hi, Liz, I think I might have an answer to that question you had …' or 'Hi Liz, I think I might have found a supplier for you …' is a heck of a lot easier to work with than 'Hi Liz, just thought we should catch up. How are you?'

- **Be upfront:** If you've put off getting in touch time and again until it seems insurmountable, the easiest way to puncture the anxiety of re-connecting is to be open about it. And that goes for a new or old contact. Be the first to say 'I've left this much too long, but I'd really like to meet up again.'

- **Do lunch:** Face to face is easier. It's more fun. And there's food.

Introductions enrich your network

Is there a weak tie at the very edge of your network who knows someone you'd like to know? Be brave and ask for an introduction.

Asking for introductions

■ **Askers usually get:** Now is the time to drop the childhood lesson that 'askers never get'. In business, you'll get nowhere by passively allowing things to happen – you have to make them happen for yourself.

■ **You deserve it:** If you've been networking effectively, the contact you've appealed to for an onward introduction should already have received considerable help and value from you: you are not being unrealistically demanding.

■ **Couch your request in mutual benefit:** A request like 'Do you think you could introduce me to Michael Connor?' relies on the unconditional generosity of your contact to do it for you. Instead, rephrase to: 'Do you think you could introduce me to Michael Connor? I'm looking at outsourcing our IT to a company like his.' Your middleman is then placed in the happy position of offering value to the two contacts on either side of him. One gets the introduction he needs, the other gets a potentially lucrative client, the guy in the middle gets to look and feel magnanimous and informed.

Making mutual introductions by email

What's the right way to go about introductions? How you handle introductions can have a profound effect on how efficiently the resulting relationships get off the ground – if at all. Let's look closely at introducing people over email – probably the most common medium for this activity.

■ **Always check you can give out contact details:** If you spot an opportunity for an existing contact and want to introduce them to someone by email, ensure – before you do anything – that you have their permission to share their contact information. This even applies to those 'once in a lifetime' opportunities where your gut instinct is to work quickly and check later. Don't. Always check with your contact first.

■ **Ensure that both parties know why they are being introduced:** You can't introduce two strangers and expect them to telepathically know how they are relevant to each other. You must explain to each of them why you think they could work together. Do so before the introduction (perhaps in a phone call), or as part of the email introduction itself, or – ideally – both.

■ **Make the transaction as easy as possible:** Everyone is busy these days. Ensure that your mutual introductions have clarity of purpose and are easy to handle for all parties. See pages 118 and 119 for details. If you burden contacts with complicated introductions that create extra work, you'll inevitably cause resentment all round.

Sounding Pro: Mutual introductions by email

Let's now take a look at what that email of mutual introduction might actually look like. While this is only one of the many ways to introduce people over email, several key features are present that should be considered every time you make such a mutual introduction.

From: *Richard Ford*
To: *Sandra Lamont*
CC: *Mike McGill*
Subject: *Sandra meet Mike, Mike meet Sandra: business opportunity*

Hi Sandra,

I know you are looking for exceptional people in design to appear in your business directory – I hope things are going well on it. With that project in mind, I'd like to introduce you to Mike McGill, who's been head of the multimedia design company Iris for the past six years. Mike is an award-winning designer who has worked on a number of high-profile multimedia marketing campaigns including the Olympic bid, Visit Britain, Recycle for Life and much more. We've known each other since University and often work together still.

Mike, Sandra is a photographer with the magazine Business Tomorrow. *She is an outstanding photographer who captures people and products at their most striking, and is currently working on a visual directory for the magazine's summer supplement. She particularly wants to meet and photograph cutting-edge designers with examples of their most unique work, which made me think about the latest additions to your portfolio.*

Sandra, perhaps you could get in touch with Mike over email to arrange a meeting if appropriate?

Thanks both, and have a great weekend.

Best regards,
Rich

The features of written introduction

The email looks simple, but the introducer has used several important tactics. Adopting these strategies can make mutual introductions easy and effective. Alongside these specific tactics, don't forget the basics of business writing that we learned in Step 3: be professional but relaxed, check your spelling and grammar, and avoid slang.

- **Acknowledge 'status':** The email is CC'd to the person who is perceived as more 'important' in terms of the transaction. This gives them an indication that they need do nothing other than wait to be contacted. By all means put both people in the 'to' line, but if you want to make it clear who does or doesn't need to act, then the CC line can suggest this with courtesy.

- **Describe exactly what is needed:** Paragraph two explains exactly what Sandra wants, and what will be expected of Mike.

- **Promote the skills of both people:** The email reveals that both people are exceptional representatives of their field. This makes both parties more confident about working with one another, and suggests that they may be of mutual value long term.

- **Explain the personal connection:** The email underlines what personal connections exist. In this case, Richard underlines his personal connection to Mike, giving Sandra confidence about making the first move.

- **Direct what to do next:** Richard is clear about what should happen next, even suggesting the best medium for this (perhaps because he knows that Mike prefers email). This direction also allows the introducer Richard to exit the transaction.

Nurture your network

Offer the help that people actually need

By now you are well-acquainted with the fact that maintaining your network relies on the 'pay it forward' mentality of offering help that is both of value to your contacts and makes them feel valued. But what do you have to give?

- **Understand your unique skills:** What do you do better than anyone? What do you know more about than anyone? Your expertise is possibly the best commodity you can offer. This includes your non-work skills too.

- **Get to know your contacts interests:** Find out what your contacts are interested in and send them related information. Tell them about approaching events in that field. You needn't restrict it just to business – showing that you care beyond your work lives can further develop professional relationships.

- **Understand your contacts' goals:** Knowing what someone hopes to achieve by when will make your help timely and appropriate.

- **Commit and follow through:** Be definite, and make it sound simple: 'I can proofread your report for you. Why not send it to me once you're finished, I'll check it over the weekend, and have it back to you Monday?' Give people a simple path to receiving help and they will follow it gratefully.

Promote yourself as a helper

You might think, 'If I'm offering all this help, when will I get anything done? And what about me?' It's understandable to feel that way, but the time and effort you put into helping now will pay dividends later – it's an investment. If you are seen as someone who habitually and unconditionally helps other people, people will want to network with you and through you. Having seen you in action, others will have confidence in introducing you onward to their own ties, giving you a ready-made bridge to other pools of talented people and fresh networks. Giving time now will save much more time later.

Receive help gratefully

It's an endearing aspect of human nature that most people enjoy helping others. If someone offers unsolicited help, don't assume that they have a hidden agenda; they may simply feel in your debt or genuinely want to offer something unconditionally. Be grateful and sincere – freely allowing yourself to be helped can make everyone feel good and enhance your working relationship.

Ask for help

If you genuinely need help, and don't make a habit of doing so, then asking for help occasionally can be a surprisingly positive action for you and your network. Be clear about what you need, so that others can identify immediately whether they can help or not without wasting their time. Clarity allows your helpers to work quickly and easily too – don't burden them with a vague problem but a specific and manageable request.

Promoting, demoting, letting go

As you spend more time with the people in your network, it will be clear which relationships are mutually valuable. Periodically fine-tuning your network ensures that you rotate these people to the top of the pile, giving you the best value from your network while making the best use of your time.

When to promote contacts

Are some people a pleasant surprise? Have a few weak ties come up trumps lately with tip-offs and insights? It's time to consciously plan in more interaction with them and ensure that you give back promptly, before they feel undervalued. Prioritize face-to-face time to cement your relationship. Consider the fact that such people may soon become one of your strong ties – a true ally – in it for the long run.

When to demote contacts

You're emailing, offering help, sending articles and phoning with answers. All for nothing and it's draining. When a contact is taking without giving, it can be frustrating, but don't give up on them yet. Appeal for help on a specific subject, and see how they respond. On the basis of that, decide whether to give them the benefit of the doubt, or spend a little less time working on the relationship.

Learn to let go

If a relationship is limping along with no benefit to either of you, it may be time to let it fade. This can happen for any reason, but the good news is that you needn't announce a formal parting of ways. Just let the relationship gently erode, letting the periods between interactions lengthen until there is no more. Clinging to relationships that benefit no one is unhelpful for both of you. It holds you both back, takes up time and prevents you both from making new, more important allies. Instead, concentrate your energies on setting such contacts free to find value elsewhere, while you do the same. Networking is a vibrant process that thrives not only on fresh input, but the generous release of outdated relationships. Embracing such change can be pivotal in creating an effective network able to support you right now, and wherever you go in the future.

Key take-aways

Think about the things you will take away from Step 7 and how you will implement them.

Topic	Take-away	Implementation
Closing conversations while you have more to say	• *Keep conversations under ten minutes.* • *Ask to talk more at a later date.*	• *Try to keep details high level.* • *Be more conscious of time.* • *Ask how the other would like to be contacted.*
Swapping business cards		
Ending conversations clearly and warmly		
Thanking the people you have met		
Recording information after an event		
Creating a follow up plan		
Using introductions to broaden and enrich your network		
Making mutual introductions by email		
Nurturing your growing network		
Offering tailored help		
Promoting, demoting, and letting go of contacts		